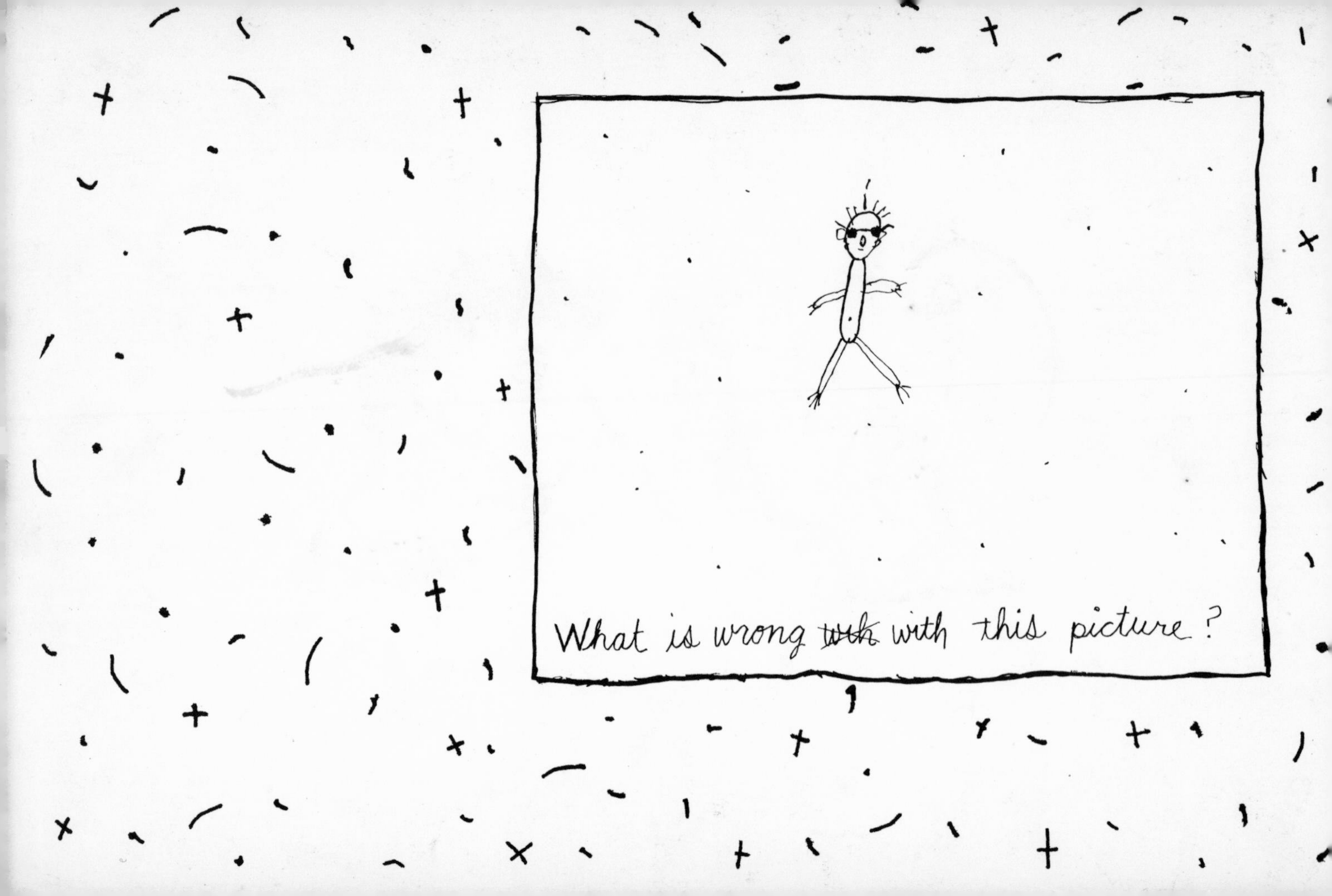
What is wrong ~~with~~ with this picture?

GIRLS AND BOYS

LYNDA BARRY

THE REAL COMET PRESS
SEATTLE

PUBLISHED BY ARRANGEMENT WITH THE AUTHOR
GIRLS AND BOYS IS AN ORIGINAL PUBLICATION OF
THE REAL COMET PRESS ←
A DIVISION OF SUCH A DEAL CORPORATION
FOR INFORMATION:
932 - 18TH AVENUE EAST
SEATTLE, WASHINGTON 98112
FIRST PRINTING → SEPTEMBER 1981
SECOND PRINTING - 1982

DESIGN BY → H. SILVERMAN + M. MICHAELSON / SQUARE STUDIO
PRINTED BY WORKSHOP PRINTERS - Seattle
FREAK FREAK, Y'ALL - ROCK THE HOUSE
ISBN 0-941104-00-1
WORK SHOP PRINTERS IU 450

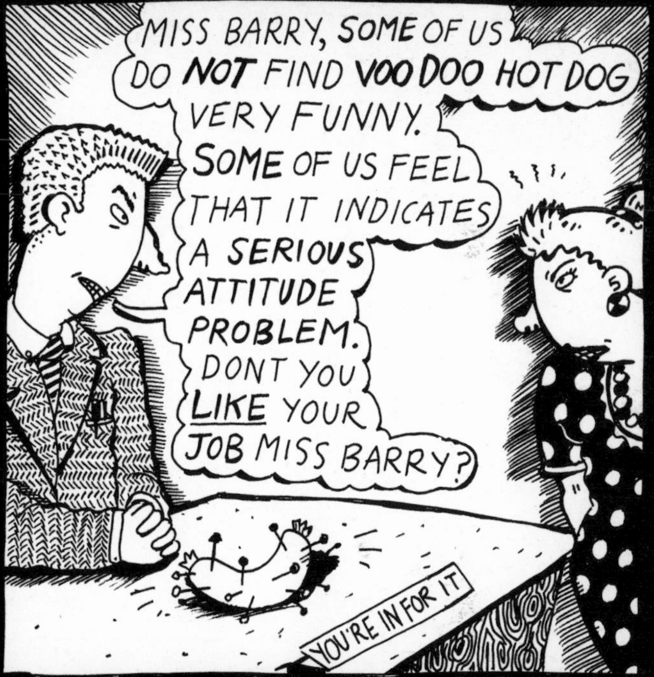
MISS BARRY, SOME OF US DO NOT FIND VOO DOO HOT DOG VERY FUNNY. SOME OF US FEEL THAT IT INDICATES A SERIOUS ATTITUDE PROBLEM. DONT YOU LIKE YOUR JOB MISS BARRY?
YOU'RE IN FOR IT

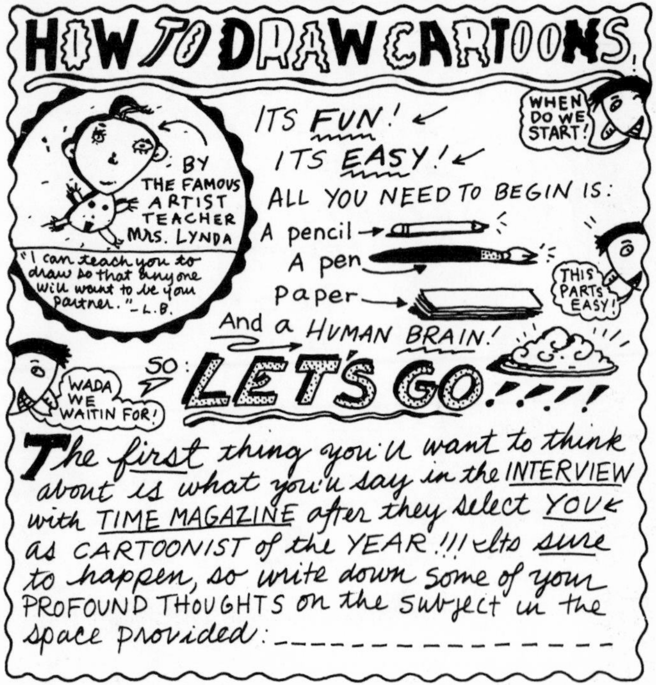
HOW TO DRAW CARTOONS
BY THE FAMOUS ARTIST TEACHER MRS. LYNDA
"I can teach you to draw so that anyone will want to be your partner." —L.B.
ITS FUN!
ITS EASY!
ALL YOU NEED TO BEGIN IS:
A pencil
A pen
Paper
And a HUMAN BRAIN!
WHEN DO WE START!
THIS PARTS EASY!
WADA WE WAITIN FOR!
SO: LET'S GO!!!!
The first thing you'll want to think about is what you'll say in the INTERVIEW with TIME MAGAZINE after they select YOU as CARTOONIST of the YEAR!!! Its sure to happen, so write down some of your PROFOUND THOUGHTS on the subject in the space provided:

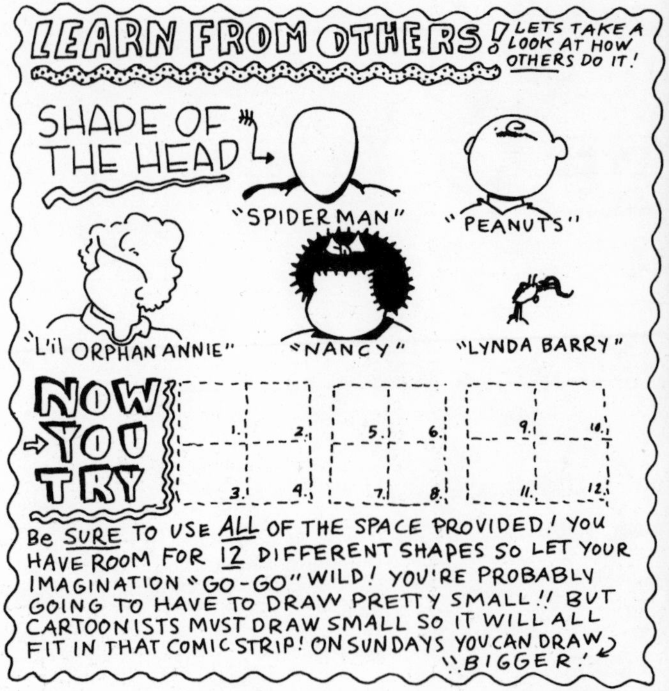
LEARN FROM OTHERS!
LETS TAKE A LOOK AT HOW OTHERS DO IT!
SHAPE OF THE HEAD
"SPIDERMAN"
"PEANUTS"
"L'il ORPHAN ANNIE"
"NANCY"
"LYNDA BARRY"
NOW YOU TRY
1. 2. 3. 4. 5. 6. 7. 8. 9. 10. 11. 12.
Be SURE TO USE ALL OF THE SPACE PROVIDED! YOU HAVE ROOM FOR 12 DIFFERENT SHAPES SO LET YOUR IMAGINATION "GO-GO" WILD! YOU'RE PROBABLY GOING TO HAVE TO DRAW PRETTY SMALL!! BUT CARTOONISTS MUST DRAW SMALL SO IT WILL ALL FIT IN THAT COMIC STRIP! ON SUNDAYS YOU CAN DRAW BIGGER!

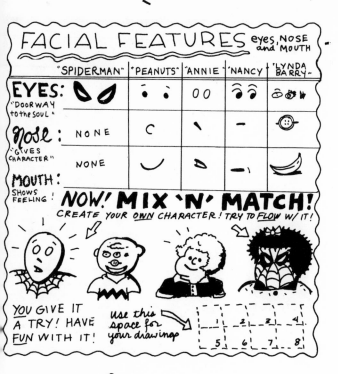

FACIAL FEATURES eyes, NOSE and MOUTH

	"SPIDERMAN"	"PEANUTS"	"ANNIE"	"NANCY"	"LYNDA BARRY"
EYES: "DOORWAY to the SOUL"	(mask eyes)	• •	0 0	(eyes)	(eyes)
nose: "GIVES CHARACTER"	NONE	C	'		(button)
MOUTH: SHOWS FEELING!	NONE	(smile)	(nose shape)	— \	(banana)

NOW! MIX 'N' MATCH!
CREATE YOUR *OWN* CHARACTER! TRY TO *FLOW* W/ IT!

YOU GIVE IT A TRY! HAVE FUN WITH IT!

Use this space for your drawings

1	2	3	4
5	6	7	8

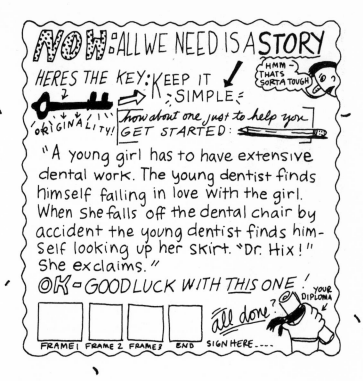

NOW: ALL WE NEED IS A STORY

HERES THE KEY: KEEP IT ↘ : SIMPLE :

ORIGINALITY!

HMM – THATS SORTA TOUGH

how about one just to help you GET STARTED :

"A young girl has to have extensive dental work. The young dentist finds himself falling in love with the girl. When she falls off the dental chair by accident the young dentist finds himself looking up her skirt. "Dr. Hix!" She exclaims."

OK – GOODLUCK WITH *THIS* ONE!

YOUR DIPLOMA

all done?

FRAME 1	FRAME 2	FRAME 3	END

SIGN HERE ----

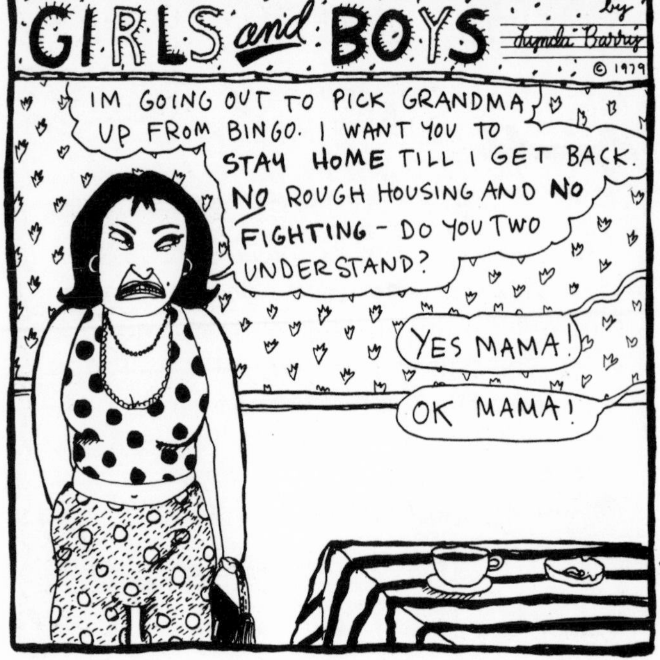
GIRLS and BOYS
by Lynda Barry
© 1979
IM GOING OUT TO PICK GRANDMA UP FROM BINGO. I WANT YOU TO STAY HOME TILL I GET BACK. NO ROUGH HOUSING AND NO FIGHTING - DO YOU TWO UNDERSTAND?
YES MAMA!
OK MAMA!

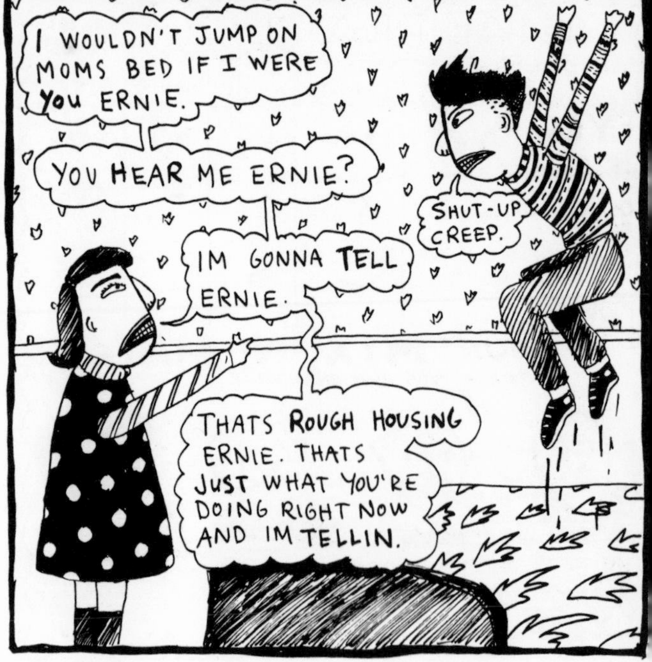
I WOULDN'T JUMP ON MOMS BED IF I WERE YOU ERNIE.
YOU HEAR ME ERNIE?
SHUT-UP CREEP.
IM GONNA TELL ERNIE.
THATS ROUGH HOUSING ERNIE. THATS JUST WHAT YOU'RE DOING RIGHT NOW AND IM TELLIN.

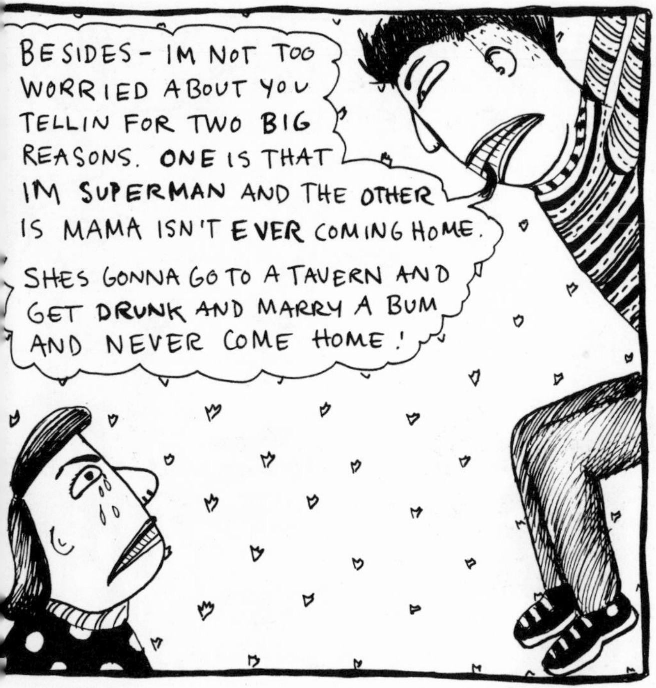
BESIDES- IM NOT TOO WORRIED ABOUT YOU TELLIN FOR TWO BIG REASONS. ONE IS THAT IM SUPERMAN AND THE OTHER IS MAMA ISN'T EVER COMING HOME.
SHES GONNA GO TO A TAVERN AND GET DRUNK AND MARRY A BUM AND NEVER COME HOME!

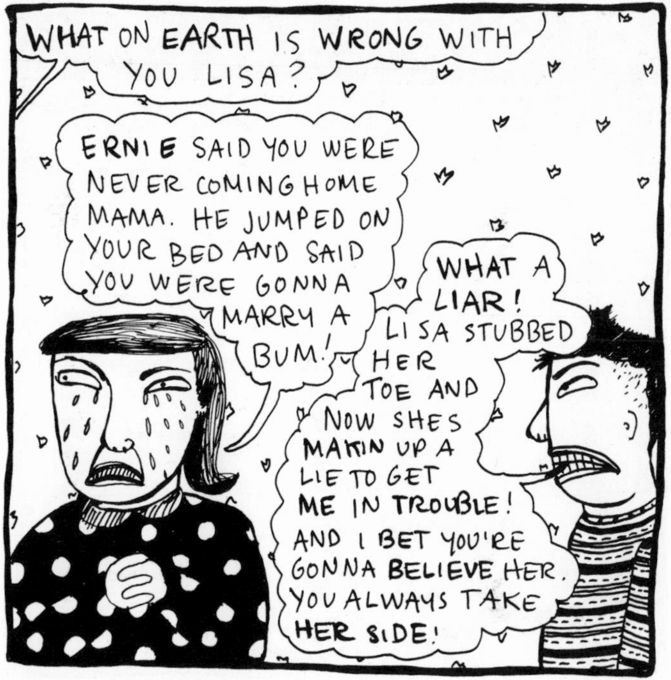
WHAT ON EARTH IS WRONG WITH YOU LISA?
ERNIE SAID YOU WERE NEVER COMING HOME MAMA. HE JUMPED ON YOUR BED AND SAID YOU WERE GONNA MARRY A BUM!
WHAT A LIAR!
LISA STUBBED HER TOE AND NOW SHES MAKIN UP A LIE TO GET ME IN TROUBLE! AND I BET YOU'RE GONNA BELIEVE HER. YOU ALWAYS TAKE HER SIDE!

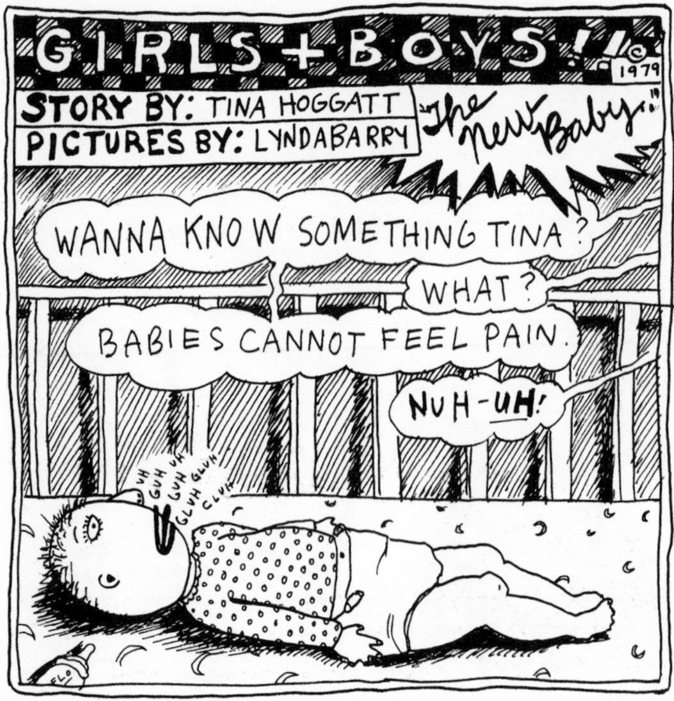
GIRLS + BOYS!! © 1979
STORY BY: TINA HOGGATT
PICTURES BY: LYNDABARRY
"The new Baby."
WANNA KNOW SOMETHING TINA?
WHAT?
BABIES CANNOT FEEL PAIN.
NUH-UH!
UH GUH UH GUH GLUH GLUH GLUH

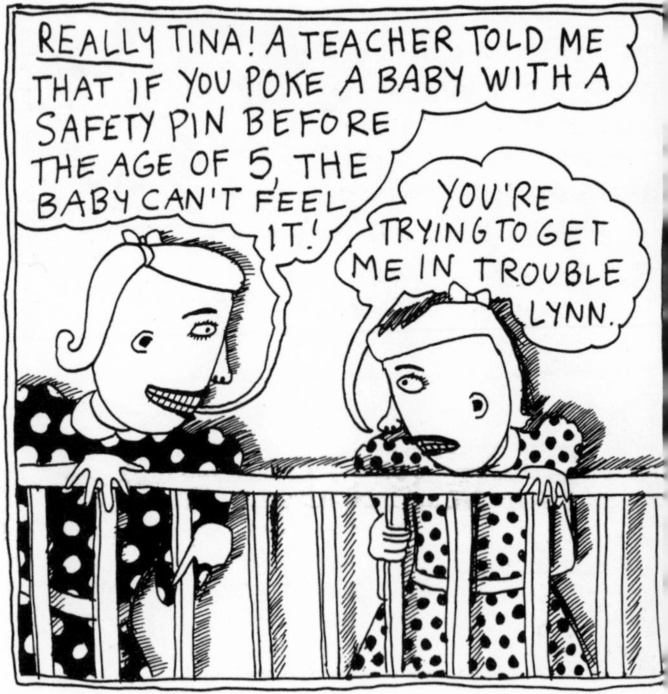
REALLY TINA! A TEACHER TOLD ME THAT IF YOU POKE A BABY WITH A SAFETY PIN BEFORE THE AGE OF 5, THE BABY CAN'T FEEL IT!
YOU'RE TRYING TO GET ME IN TROUBLE LYNN.

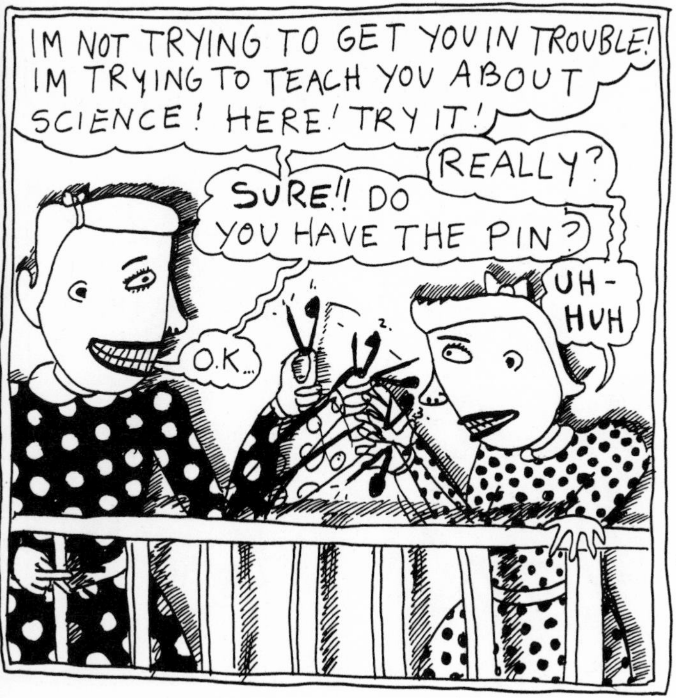
IM NOT TRYING TO GET YOU IN TROUBLE! IM TRYING TO TEACH YOU ABOUT SCIENCE! HERE! TRY IT!
REALLY?
SURE!! DO YOU HAVE THE PIN?
UH-HUH
O.K...

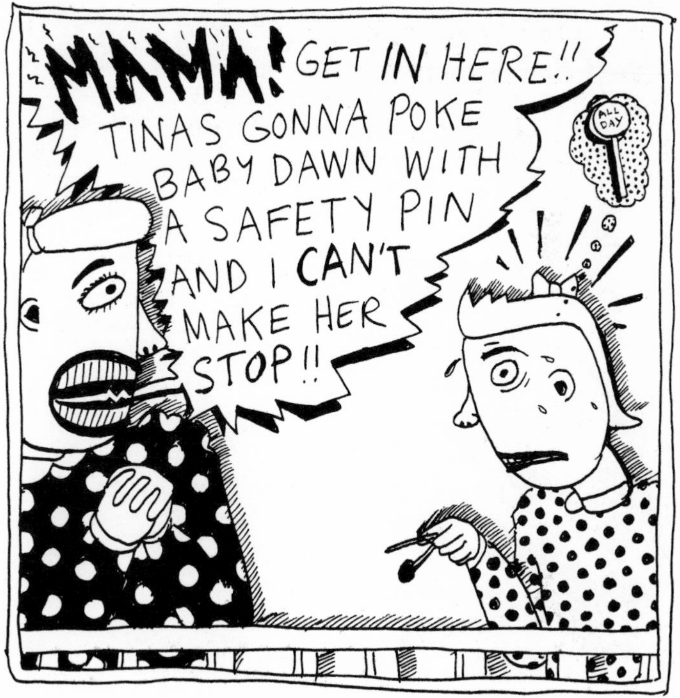
MAMA! GET IN HERE!! TINAS GONNA POKE BABY DAWN WITH A SAFETY PIN AND I CAN'T MAKE HER STOP!!
ALL DAY

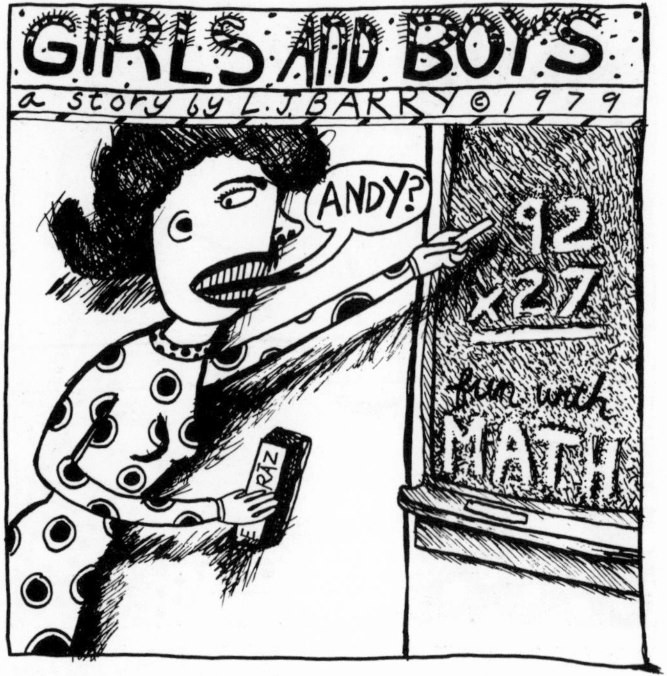
GIRLS AND BOYS
a story by L.J. BARRY © 1979
ANDY?
92
×27
fun with
MATH
RAZ

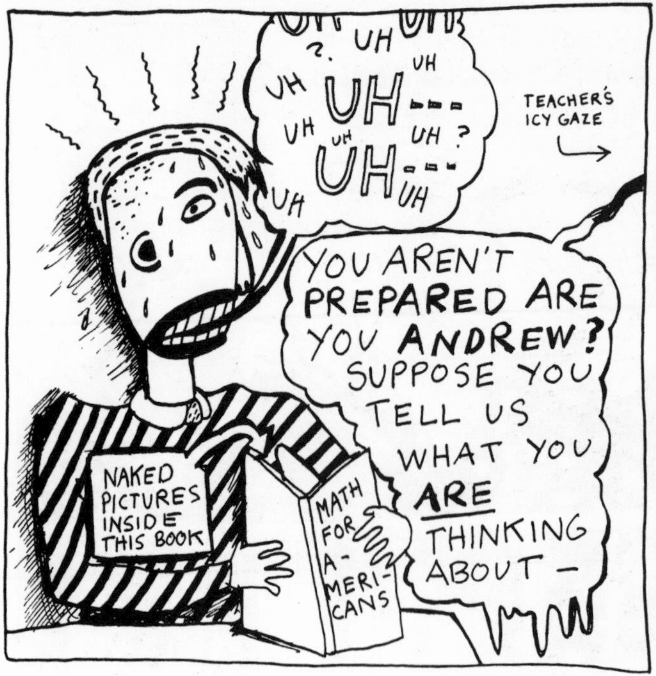
? UH
UH
UH UH
UH UH
UH ?
UH UH
UH
UH
TEACHER'S ICY GAZE
YOU AREN'T PREPARED ARE YOU ANDREW? SUPPOSE YOU TELL US WHAT YOU ARE THINKING ABOUT –
NAKED PICTURES INSIDE THIS BOOK
MATH FOR A-MERI-CANS

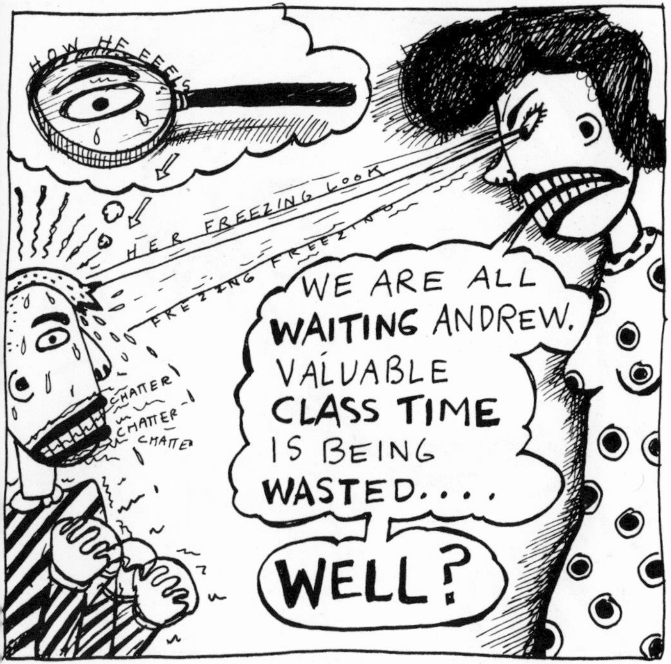
HOW HE FEELS
HER FREEZING LOOK
FREEZING FREEZING
CHATTER CHATTER CHATTER
WE ARE ALL WAITING ANDREW. VALUABLE CLASS TIME IS BEING WASTED....
WELL?

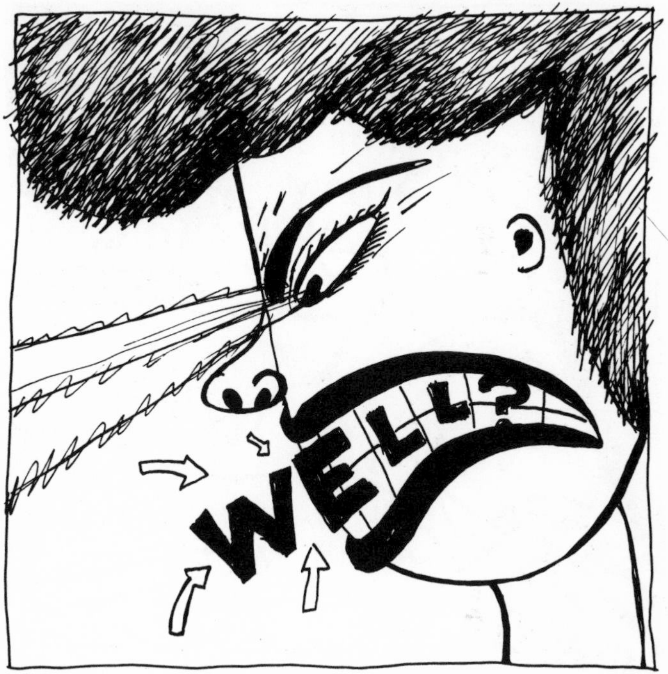
WELL?

continued

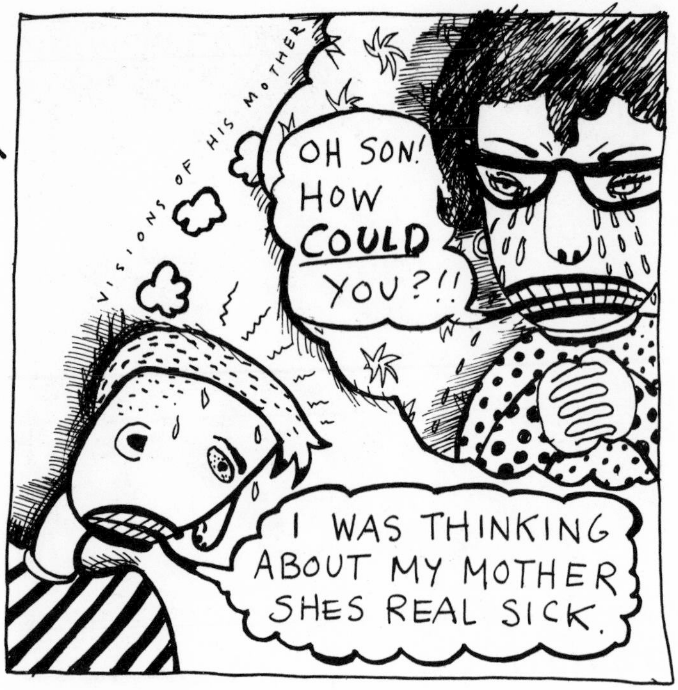
VISIONS OF HIS MOTHER
OH SON! HOW COULD YOU?!!
I WAS THINKING ABOUT MY MOTHER SHES REAL SICK.

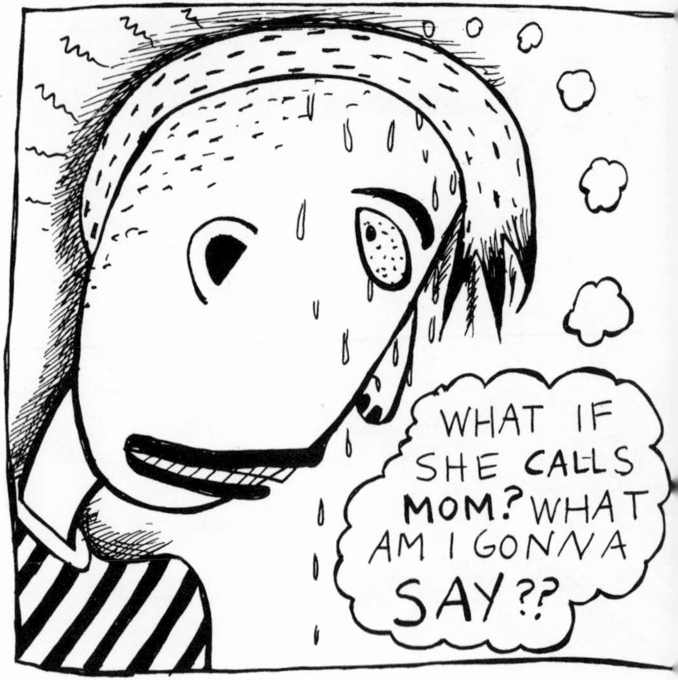
WHAT IF SHE CALLS MOM? WHAT AM I GONNA SAY??

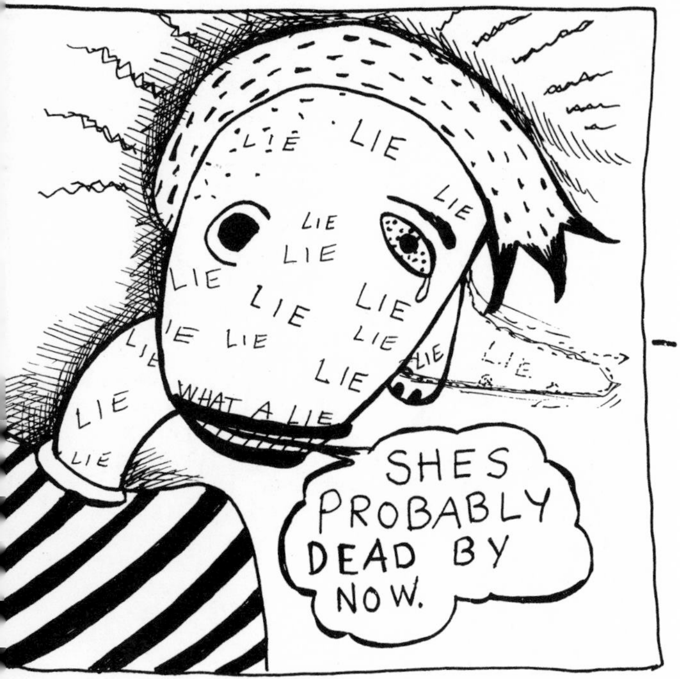
LIE LIE LIE LIE LIE LIE LIE LIE LIE LIE LIE LIE LIE LIE LIE LIE LIE
WHAT A LIE
SHES PROBABLY DEAD BY NOW.

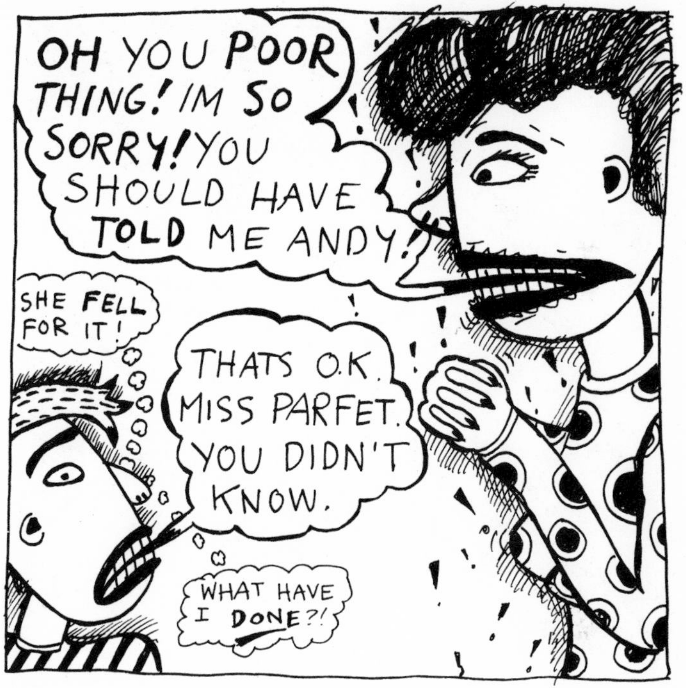
OH YOU POOR THING! IM SO SORRY! YOU SHOULD HAVE TOLD ME ANDY!
SHE FELL FOR IT!
THATS O.K. MISS PARFET. YOU DIDN'T KNOW.
WHAT HAVE I DONE?!

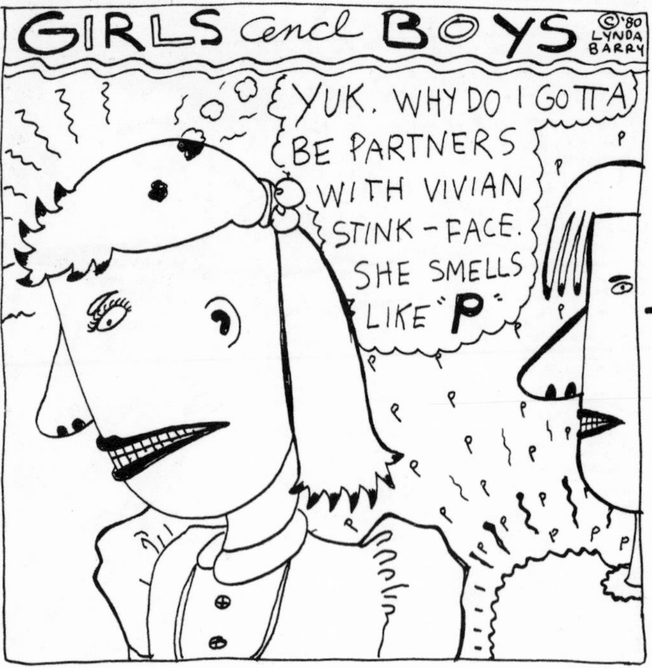

GIRLS and BOYS
©'80 LYNDA BARRY
YUK. WHY DO I GOTTA BE PARTNERS WITH VIVIAN STINK-FACE. SHE SMELLS LIKE "P"

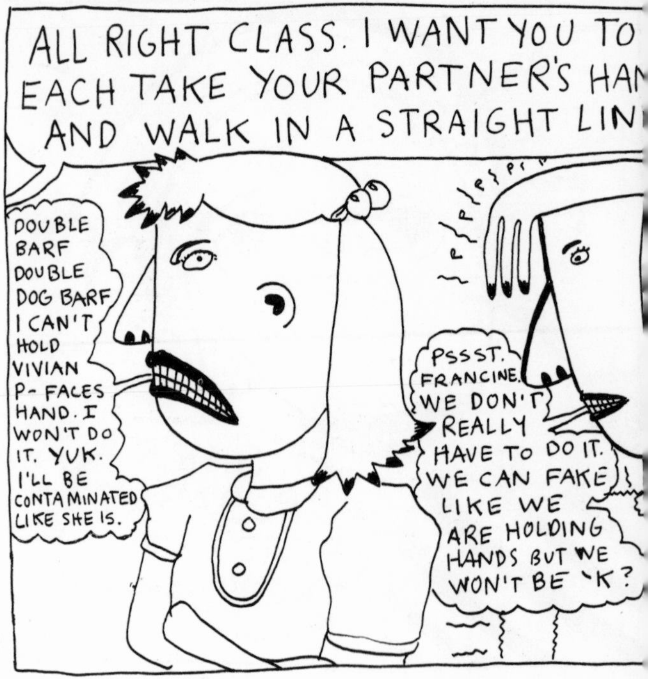

ALL RIGHT CLASS. I WANT YOU TO EACH TAKE YOUR PARTNER'S HAN AND WALK IN A STRAIGHT LIN
DOUBLE BARF DOUBLE DOUBLE DOG BARF I CAN'T HOLD VIVIAN P-FACES HAND. I WON'T DO IT. YUK. I'LL BE CONTAMINATED LIKE SHE IS.
PSSST. FRANCINE. WE DON'T REALLY HAVE TO DO IT. WE CAN FAKE LIKE WE ARE HOLDING HANDS BUT WE WON'T BE 'K?

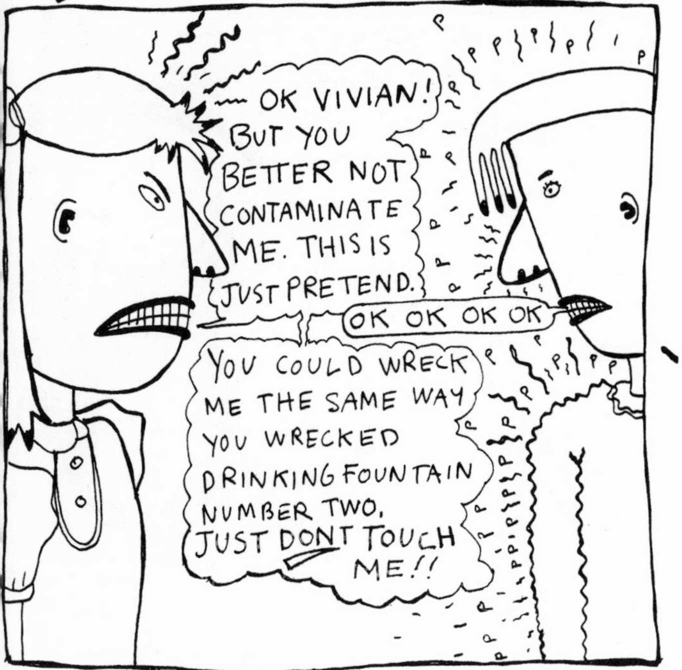
OK VIVIAN! BUT YOU BETTER NOT CONTAMINATE ME. THIS IS JUST PRETEND.
OK OK OK OK
YOU COULD WRECK ME THE SAME WAY YOU WRECKED DRINKING FOUNTAIN NUMBER TWO. JUST DONT TOUCH ME!!

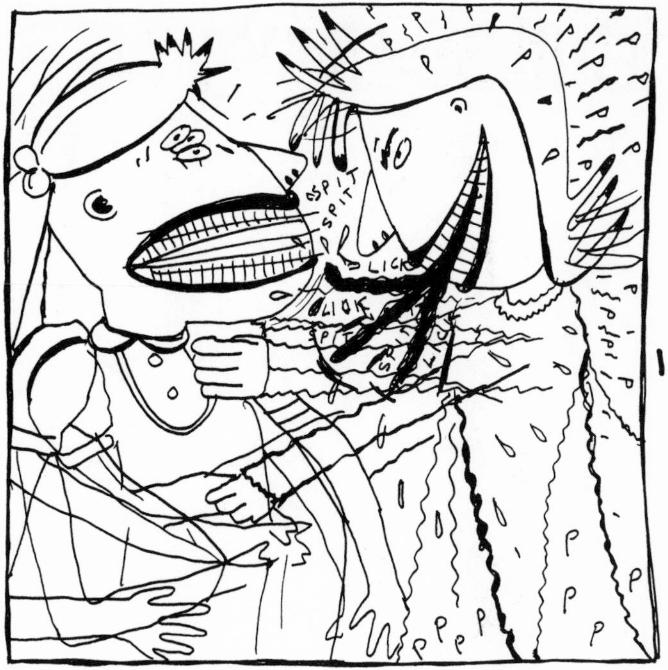
SPIT
SPIT
SPIT
LICK
LICK

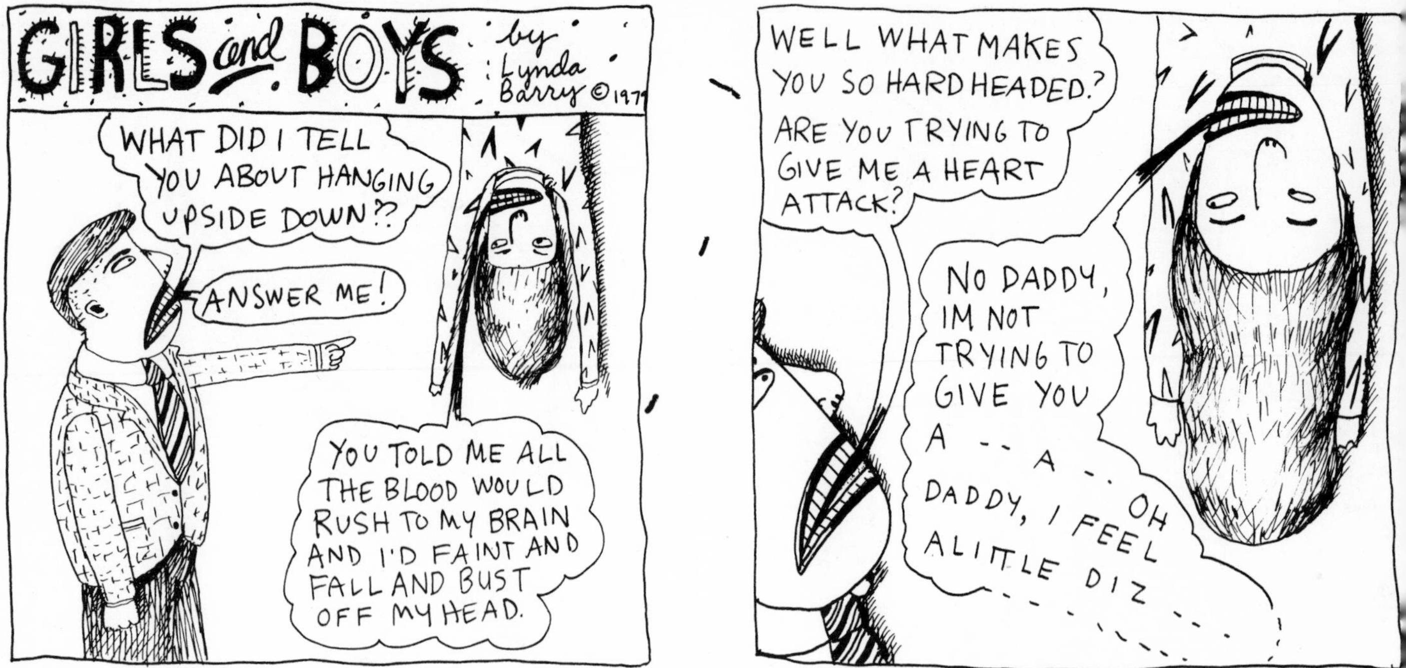
GIRLS and BOYS by Lynda Barry ©1979
WHAT DID I TELL YOU ABOUT HANGING UPSIDE DOWN??
ANSWER ME!
YOU TOLD ME ALL THE BLOOD WOULD RUSH TO MY BRAIN AND I'D FAINT AND FALL AND BUST OFF MY HEAD.
WELL WHAT MAKES YOU SO HARD HEADED? ARE YOU TRYING TO GIVE ME A HEART ATTACK?
NO DADDY, IM NOT TRYING TO GIVE YOU A -- A -- OH DADDY, I FEEL ALITTLE DIZ.......

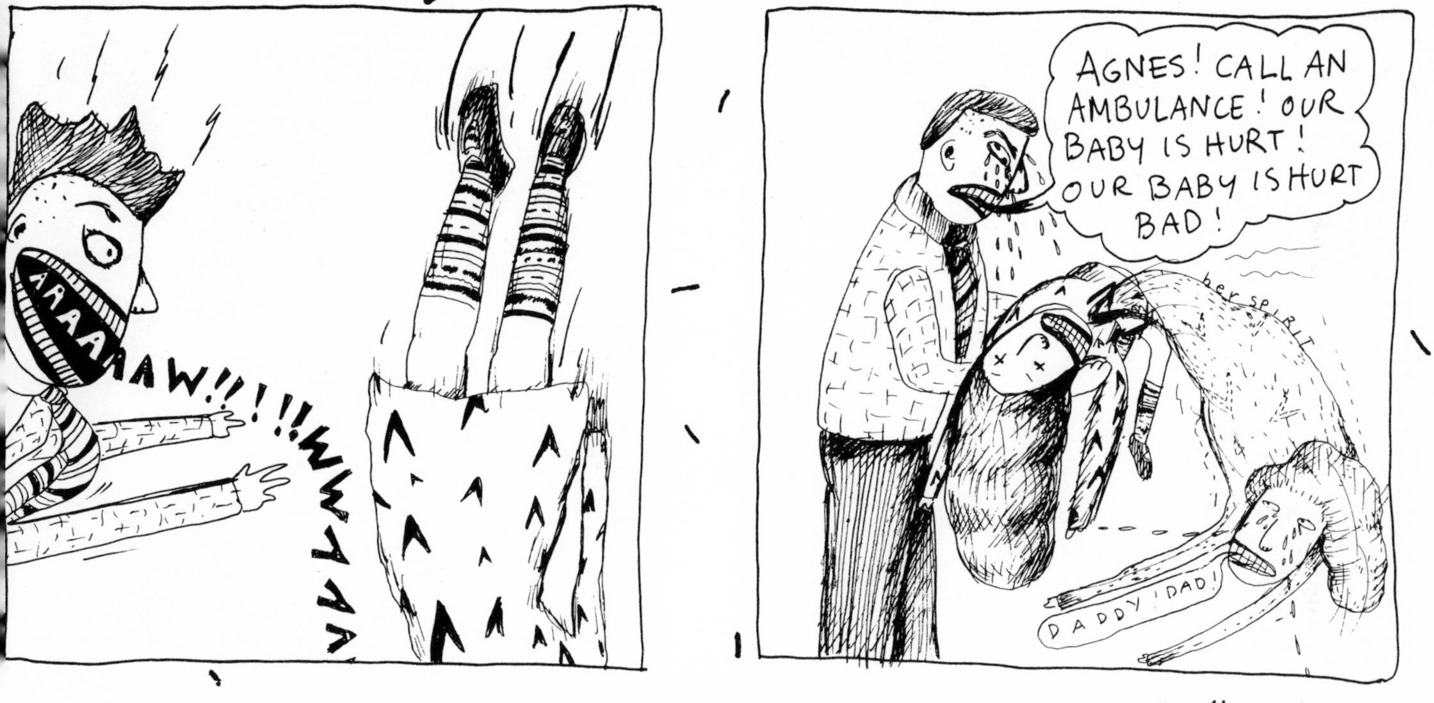
AAAAAAW!!!!!!WWAAAA
AGNES! CALL AN AMBULANCE! OUR BABY IS HURT! OUR BABY IS HURT BAD!
her SPIRIT
DADDY ! DAD!

continued

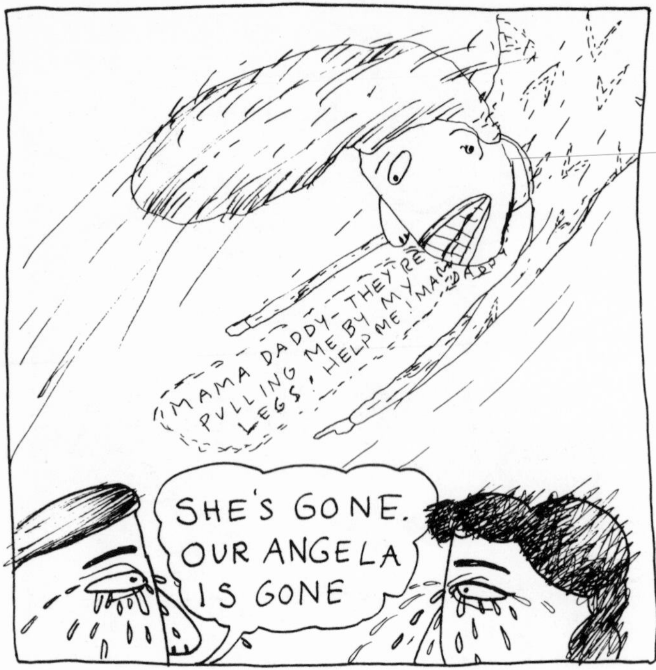
MAMA DADDY- THEY'RE PULLING ME BY MY LEGS! HELP ME!
SHE'S GONE. OUR ANGELA IS GONE

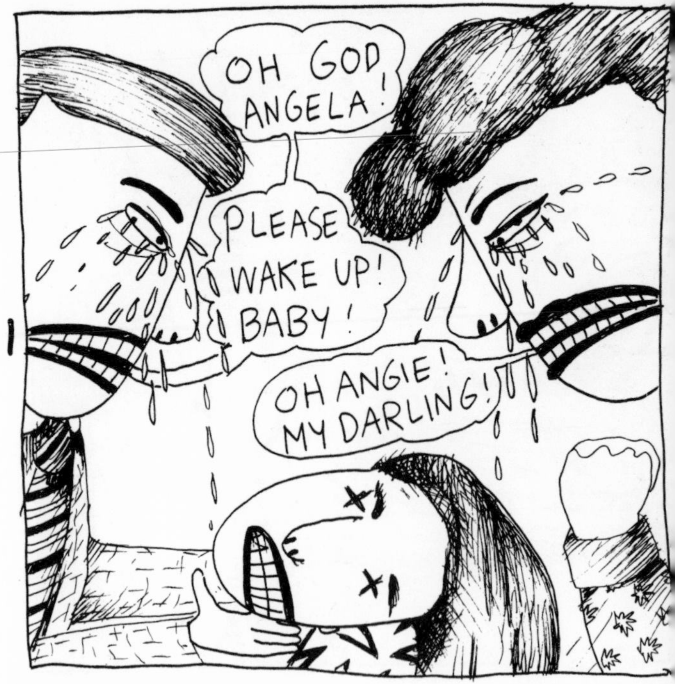
OH GOD, ANGELA!
PLEASE WAKE UP! BABY!
OH ANGIE! MY DARLING!

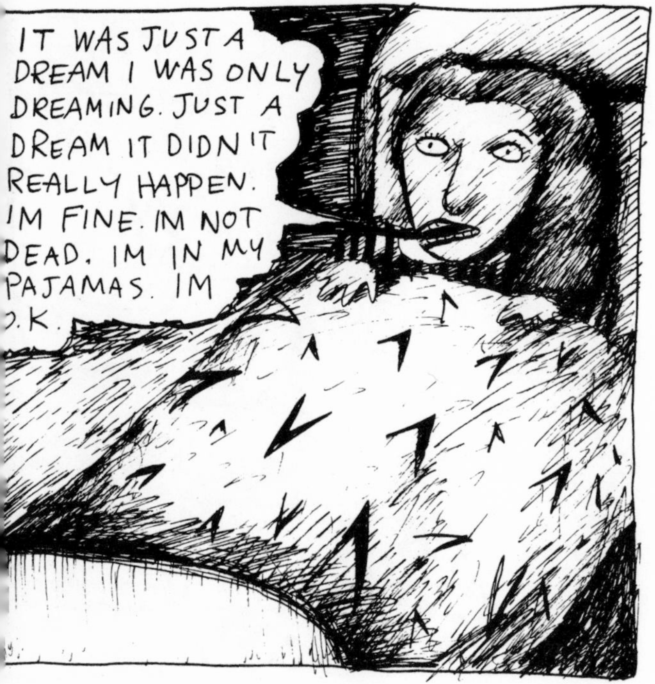
IT WAS JUST A DREAM I WAS ONLY DREAMING. JUST A DREAM IT DIDN'T REALLY HAPPEN. IM FINE. IM NOT DEAD. IM IN MY PAJAMAS. IM O.K.

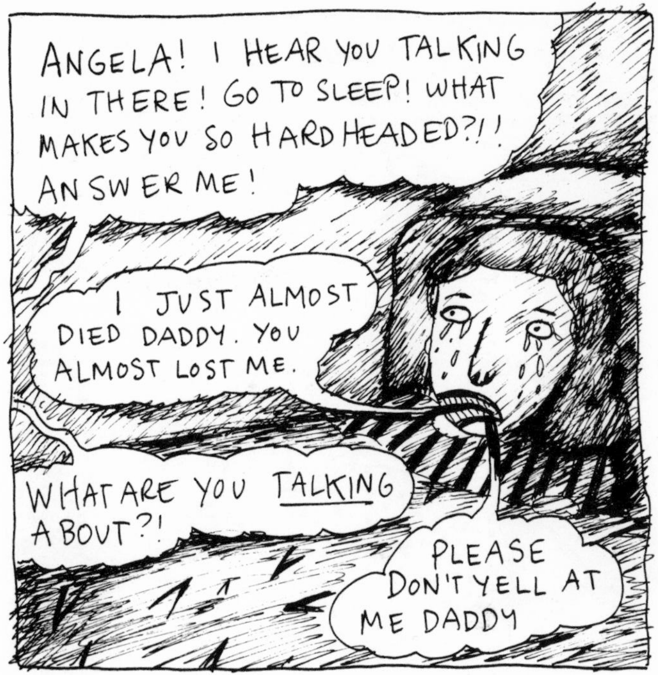
ANGELA! I HEAR YOU TALKING IN THERE! GO TO SLEEP! WHAT MAKES YOU SO HARD HEADED?!!ANSWER ME!
I JUST ALMOST DIED DADDY. YOU ALMOST LOST ME.
WHAT ARE YOU TALKING ABOUT?!
PLEASE DON'T YELL AT ME DADDY

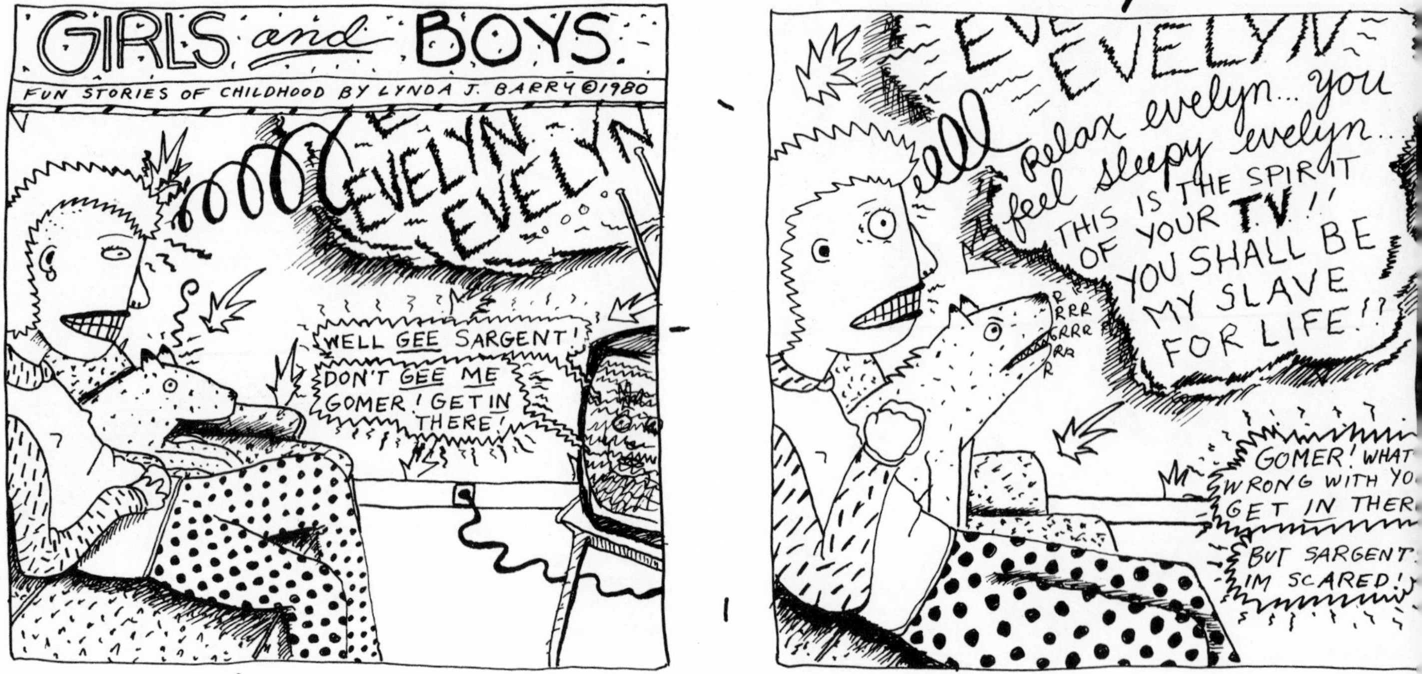
GIRLS and BOYS
FUN STORIES OF CHILDHOOD BY LYNDA J. BARRY ©1980
EVELYN EVELYN EVELYN
WELL GEE SARGENT!
DON'T GEE ME GOMER! GET IN THERE!
EVE EVELYN
Relax evelyn... you feel sleepy evelyn...
THIS IS THE SPIRIT OF YOUR TV!! YOU SHALL BE MY SLAVE FOR LIFE!!
R RRR GRRR RR R
GOMER! WHAT
WRONG WITH YO
GET IN THER
BUT SARGENT IM SCARED!

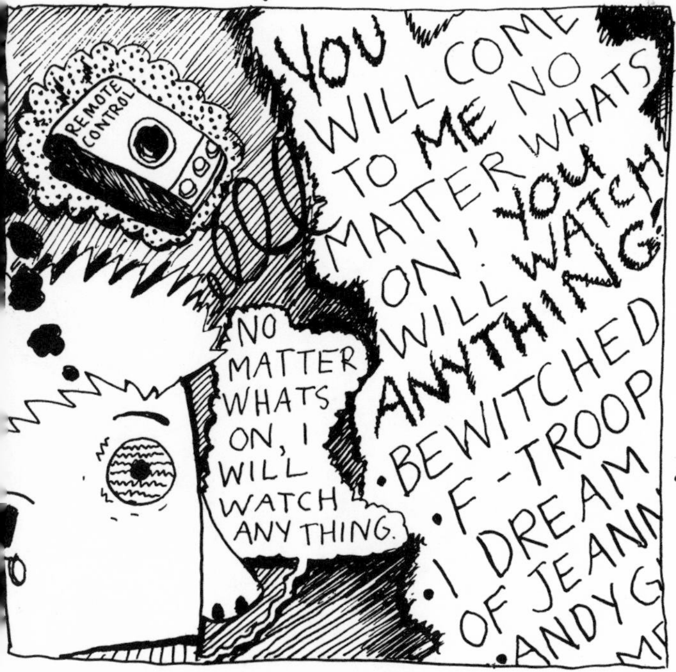
REMOTE CONTROL
YOU WILL COME TO ME NO MATTER WHATS ON, YOU WILL WATCH ANYTHING!
•BEWITCHED
•F-TROOP
•I DREAM OF JEANN
•ANDY G
NO MATTER WHATS ON, I WILL WATCH ANY THING.

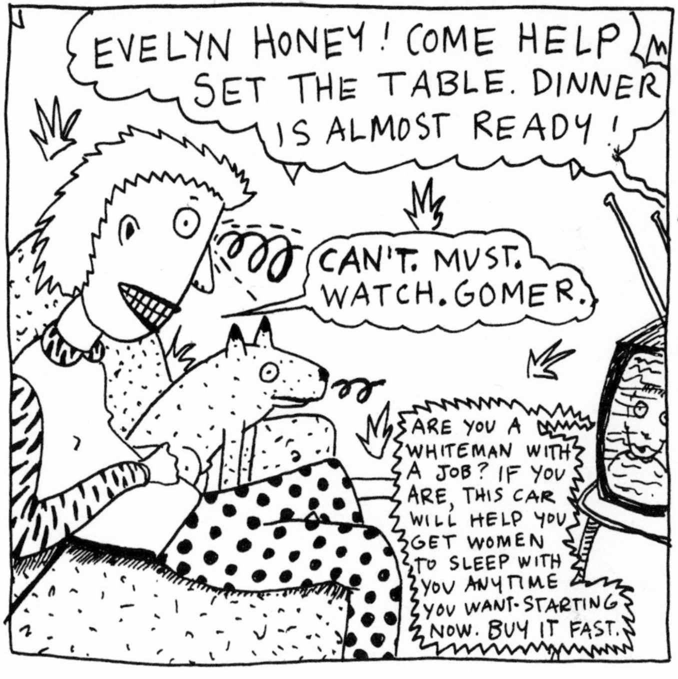
EVELYN HONEY! COME HELP SET THE TABLE. DINNER IS ALMOST READY!
CAN'T. MUST. WATCH. GOMER.
ARE YOU A WHITEMAN WITH A JOB? IF YOU ARE, THIS CAR WILL HELP YOU GET WOMEN TO SLEEP WITH YOU ANYTIME YOU WANT-STARTING NOW. BUY IT FAST.

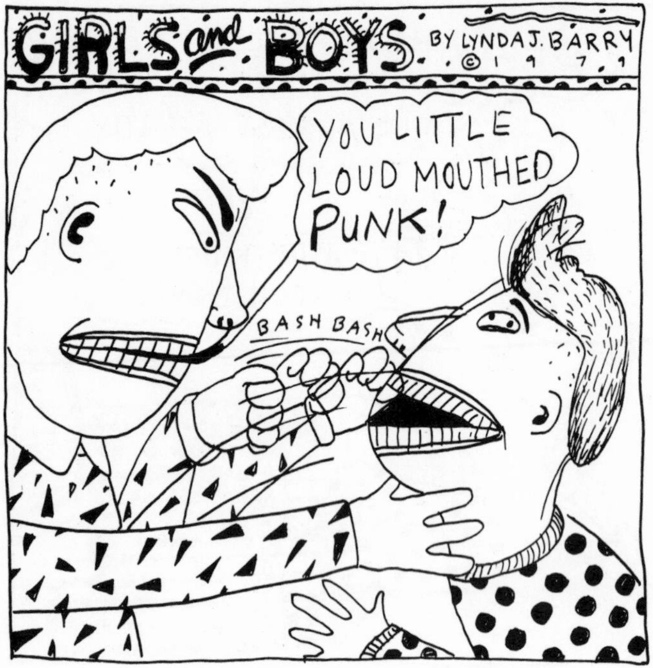
GIRLS and BOYS
BY LYNDA J. BARRY ©1977
YOU LITTLE LOUD MOUTHED PUNK!
BASH BASH

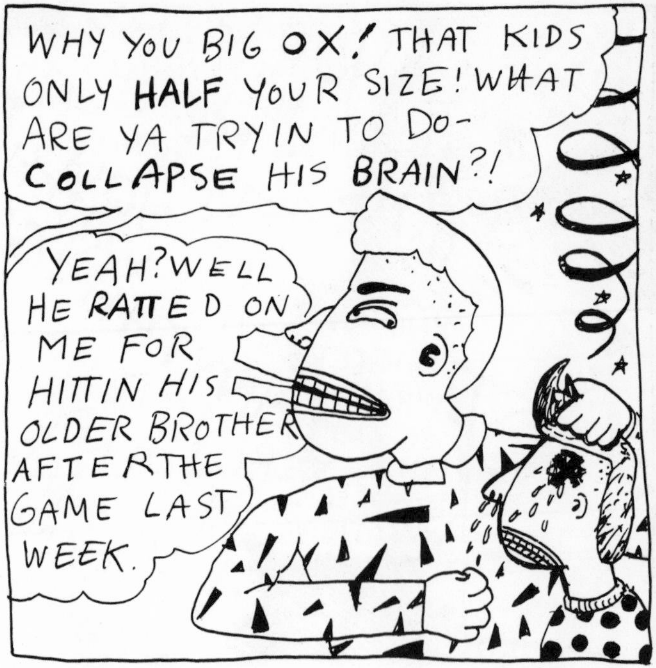
WHY YOU BIG OX! THAT KIDS ONLY HALF YOUR SIZE! WHAT ARE YA TRYIN TO DO- COLLAPSE HIS BRAIN?!
YEAH? WELL HE RATTED ON ME FOR HITTIN HIS OLDER BROTHER AFTER THE GAME LAST WEEK.

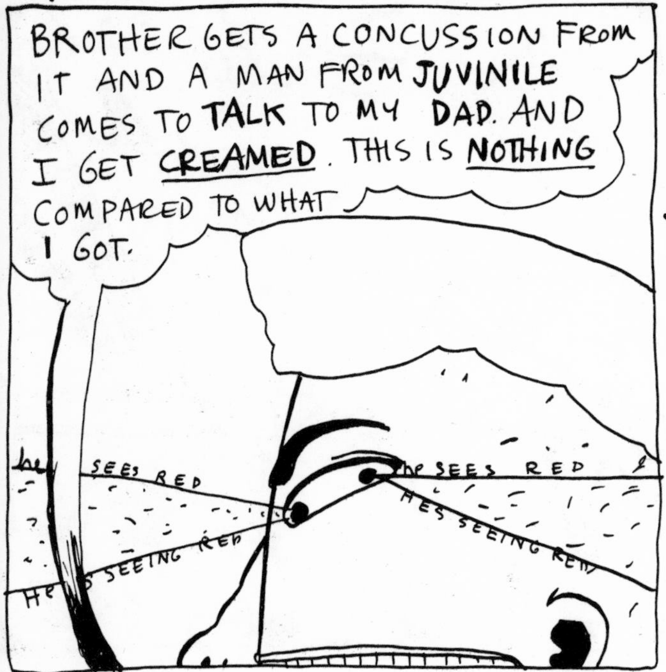
BROTHER GETS A CONCUSSION FROM IT AND A MAN FROM JUVINILE COMES TO TALK TO MY DAD. AND I GET CREAMED. THIS IS NOTHING COMPARED TO WHAT I GOT.
he SEES RED
he SEES RED
HES SEEING RED
HES SEEING RED

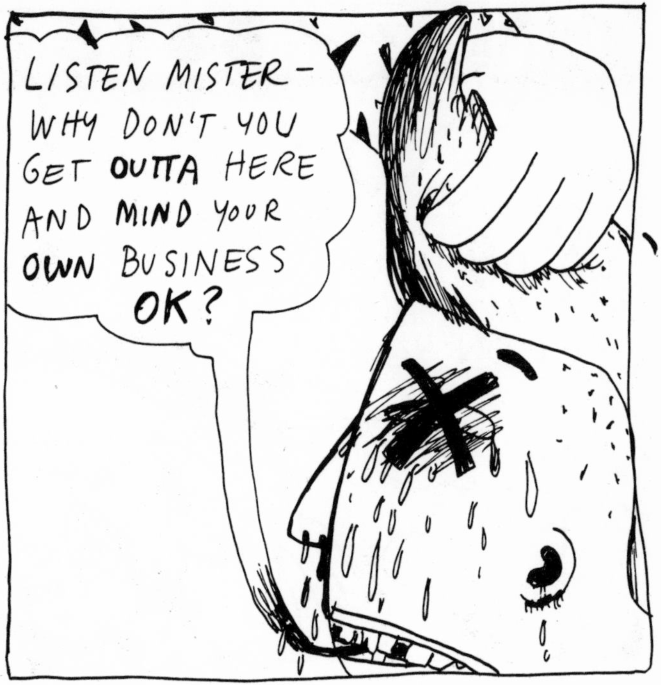
LISTEN MISTER- WHY DON'T YOU GET OUTTA HERE AND MIND YOUR OWN BUSINESS OK?

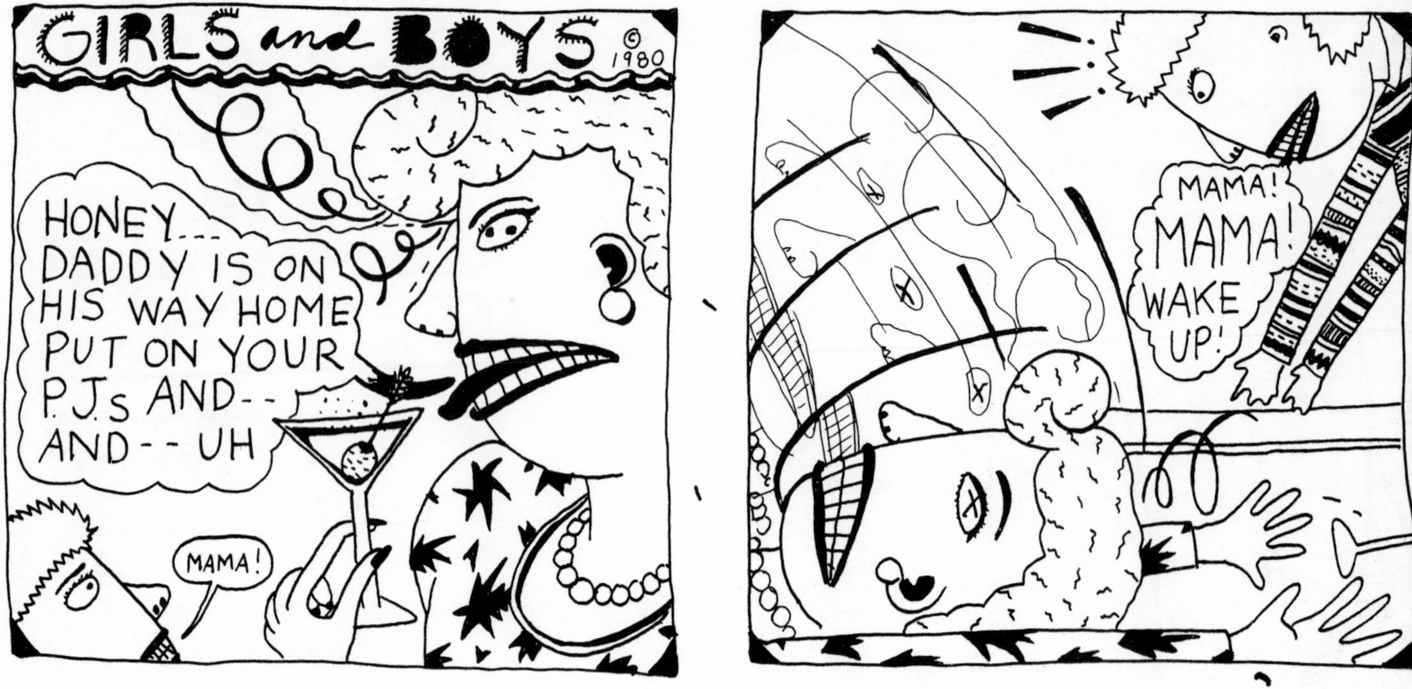
GIRLS and BOYS © 1980
HONEY... DADDY IS ON HIS WAY HOME PUT ON YOUR P.J.s AND-- AND-- UH
MAMA!
MAMA! MAMA! WAKE UP!

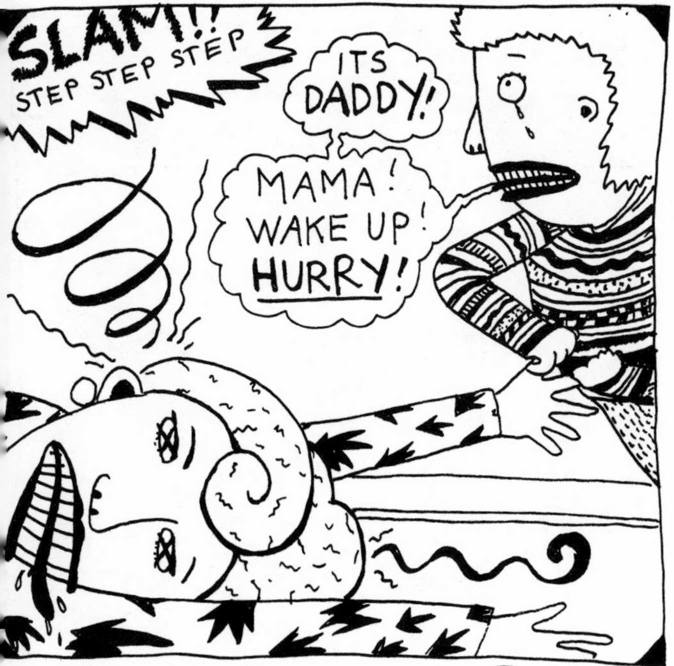
SLAM!!
STEP STEP STEP STEP
ITS DADDY!
MAMA! WAKE UP! HURRY!

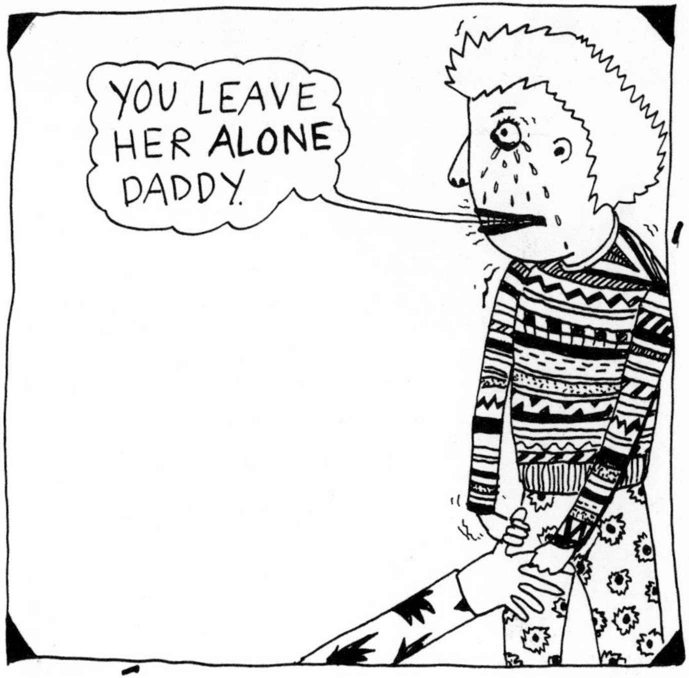
YOU LEAVE HER ALONE DADDY.

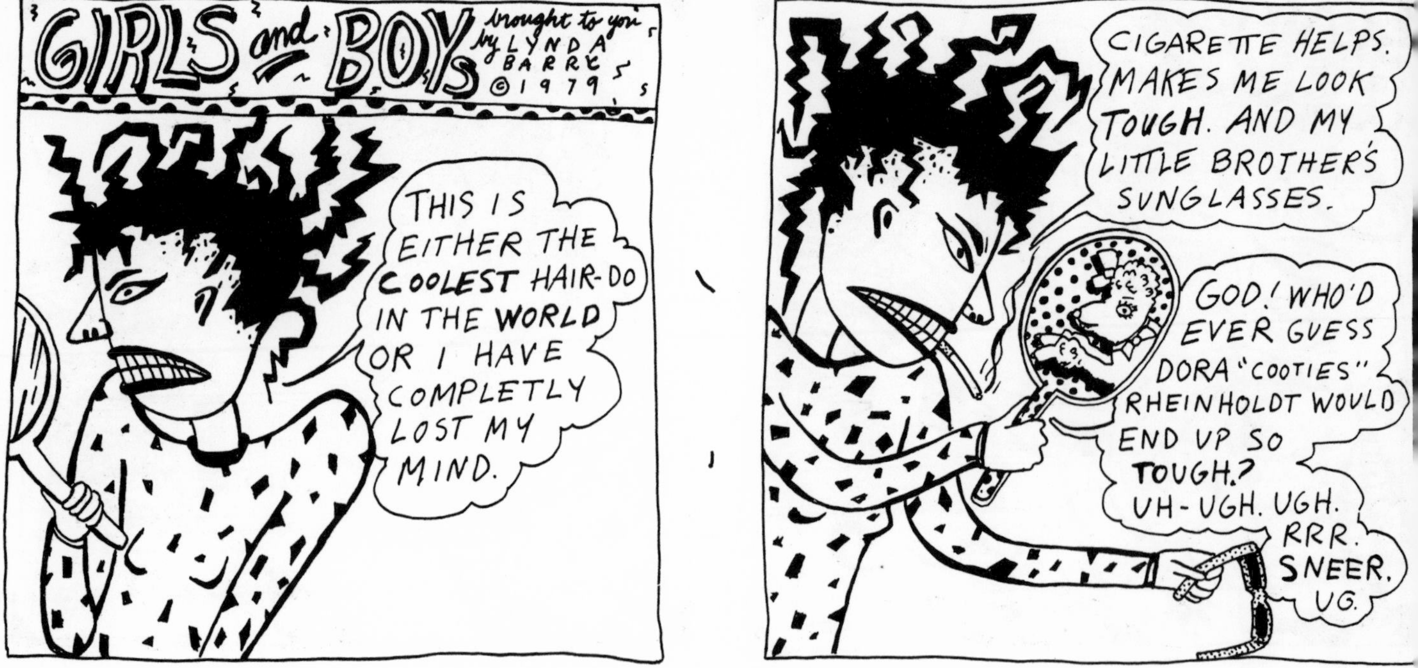
GIRLS and BOYS
brought to you by LYNDA BARRY ©1979
THIS IS EITHER THE COOLEST HAIR-DO IN THE WORLD OR I HAVE COMPLETLY LOST MY MIND.
CIGARETTE HELPS. MAKES ME LOOK TOUGH. AND MY LITTLE BROTHER'S SUNGLASSES.
GOD! WHO'D EVER GUESS DORA "COOTIES" RHEINHOLDT WOULD END UP SO TOUGH.? UH-UGH. UGH. RRR. SNEER. UG.

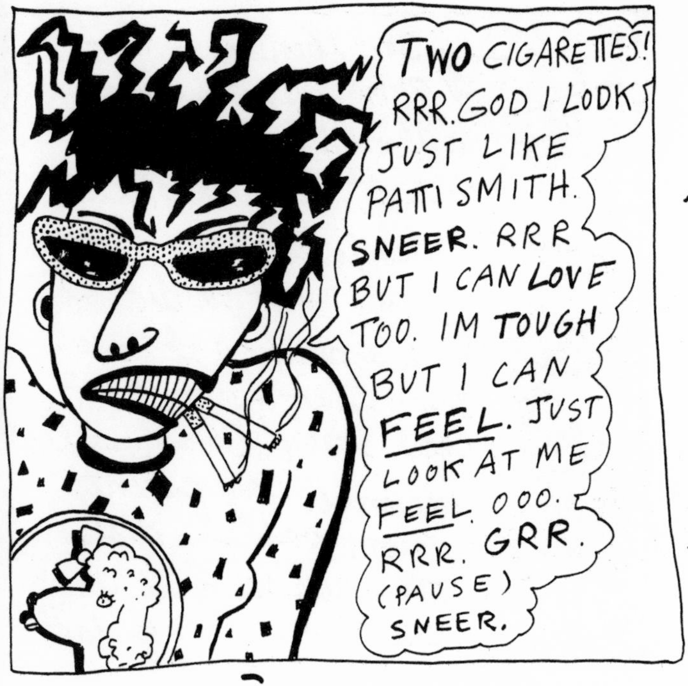
TWO CIGARETTES! RRR. GOD I LOOK JUST LIKE PATTI SMITH. SNEER. RRR BUT I CAN LOVE TOO. IM TOUGH BUT I CAN FEEL. JUST LOOK AT ME FEEL OOO. RRR. GRR. (PAUSE) SNEER.

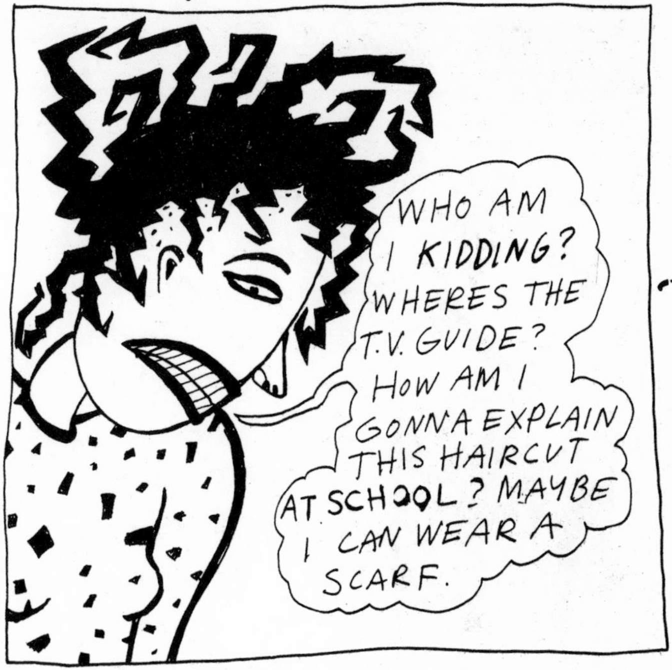
WHO AM I KIDDING? WHERES THE T.V. GUIDE? HOW AM I GONNA EXPLAIN THIS HAIRCUT AT SCHOOL? MAYBE I CAN WEAR A SCARF.

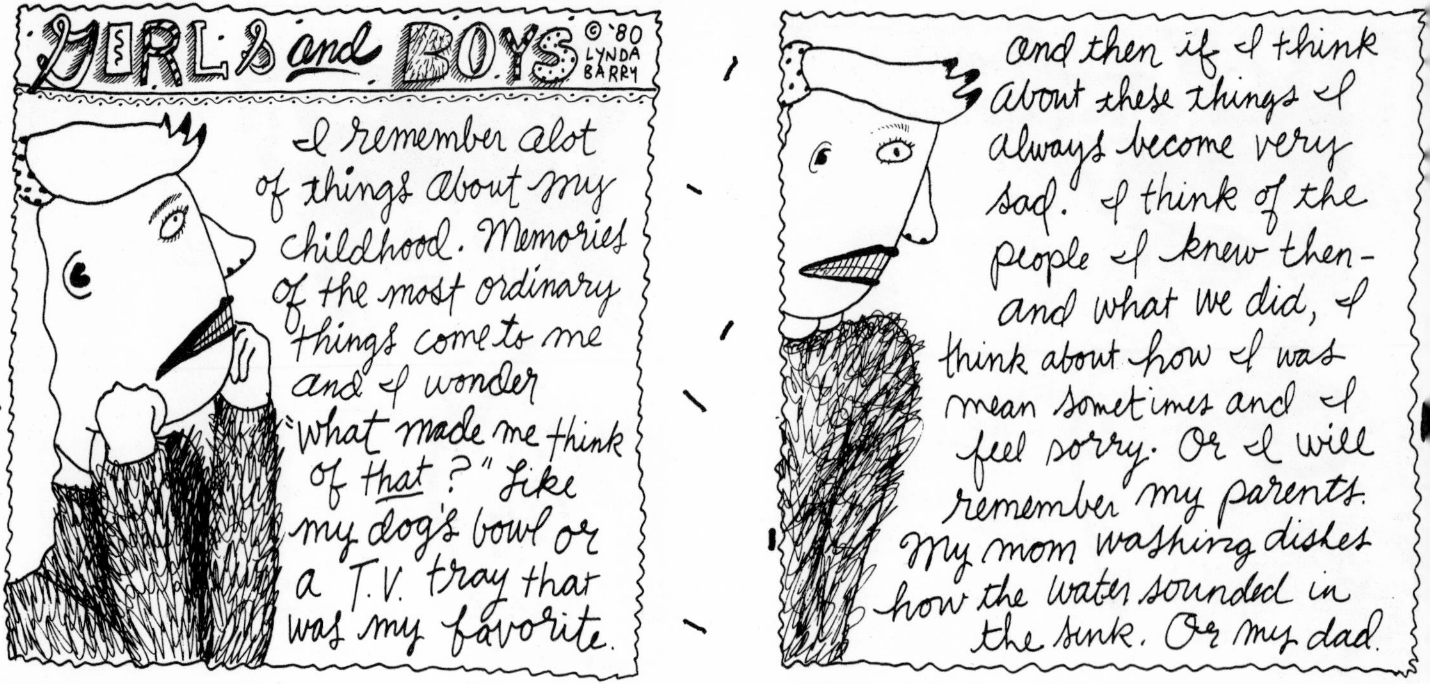
GIRLS and BOYS
© '80 LYNDA BARRY
I remember alot of things about my childhood. Memories of the most ordinary things come to me and I wonder "What made me think of that?" Like my dog's bowl or a T.V. tray that was my favorite.
and then if I think about these things I always become very sad. I think of the people I knew then— and what we did, I think about how I was mean sometimes and I feel sorry. Or I will remember my parents. My mom washing dishes how the water sounded in the sink. Or my dad.

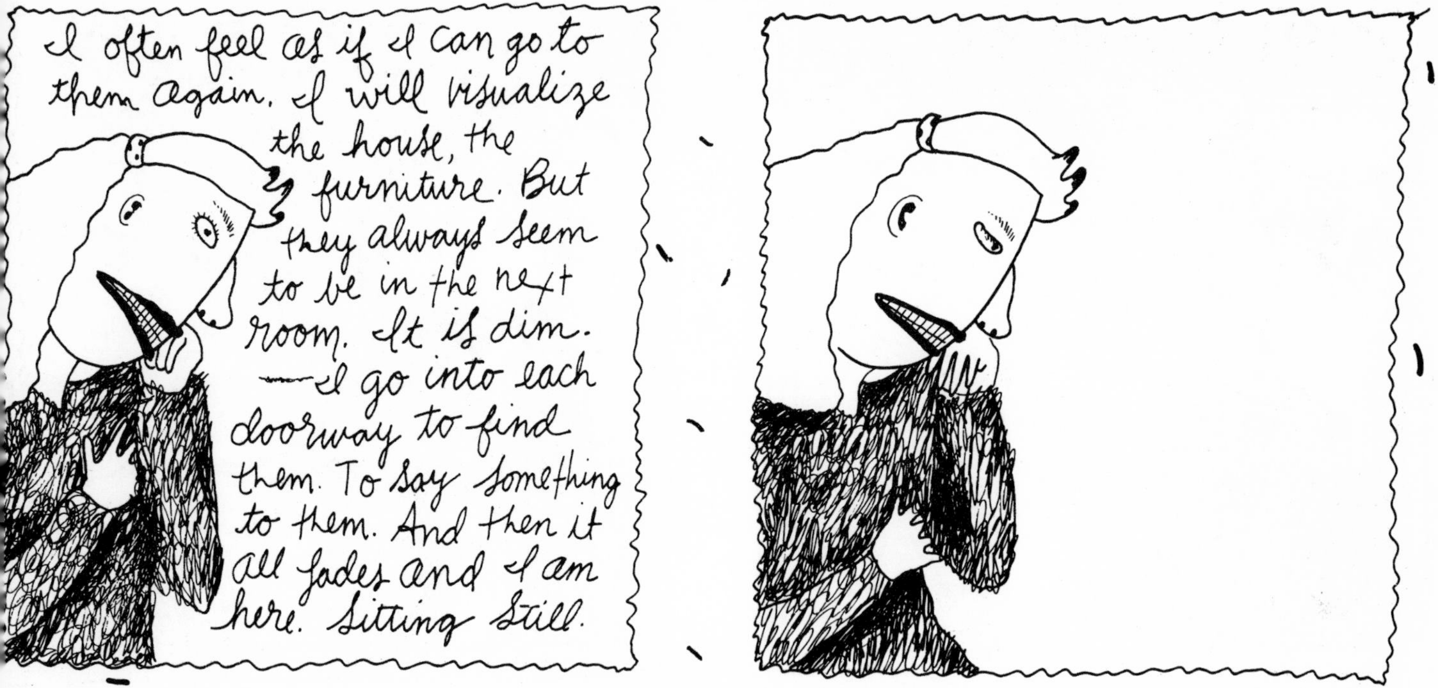
I often feel as if I can go to them again. I will visualize the house, the furniture. But they always seem to be in the next room. It is dim. —I go into each doorway to find them. To say something to them. And then it all fades and I am here. Sitting still.

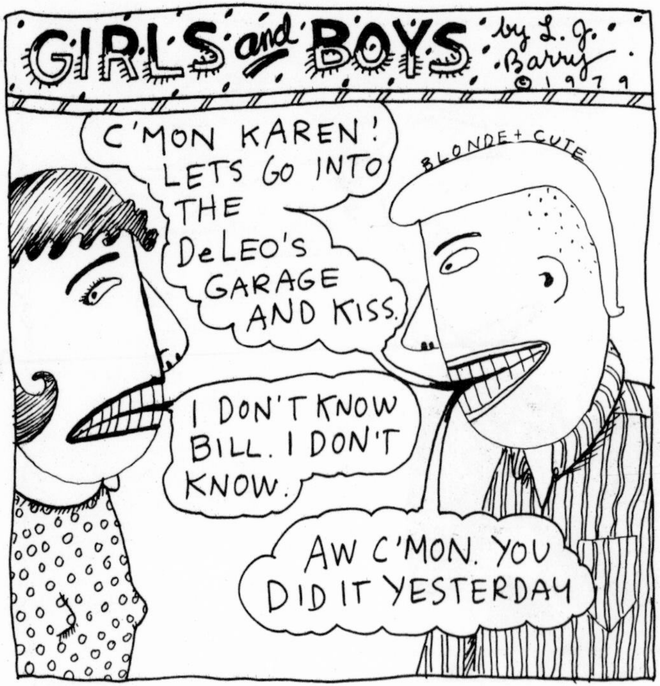
GIRLS and BOYS
by L. J. Barry ©1979
C'MON KAREN! LETS GO INTO THE DeLEO'S GARAGE AND KISS.
BLONDE + CUTE
I DON'T KNOW BILL. I DON'T KNOW.
AW C'MON. YOU DID IT YESTERDAY

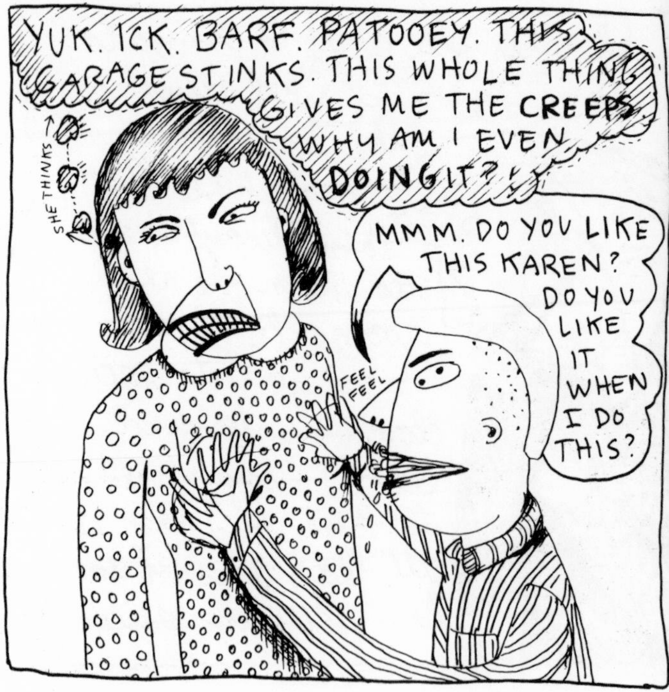
YUK. ICK. BARF. PATOOEY. THIS GARAGE STINKS. THIS WHOLE THING GIVES ME THE CREEPS. WHY AM I EVEN DOING IT?!
SHE THINKS
MMM. DO YOU LIKE THIS KAREN? DO YOU LIKE IT WHEN I DO THIS?
FEEL FEEL

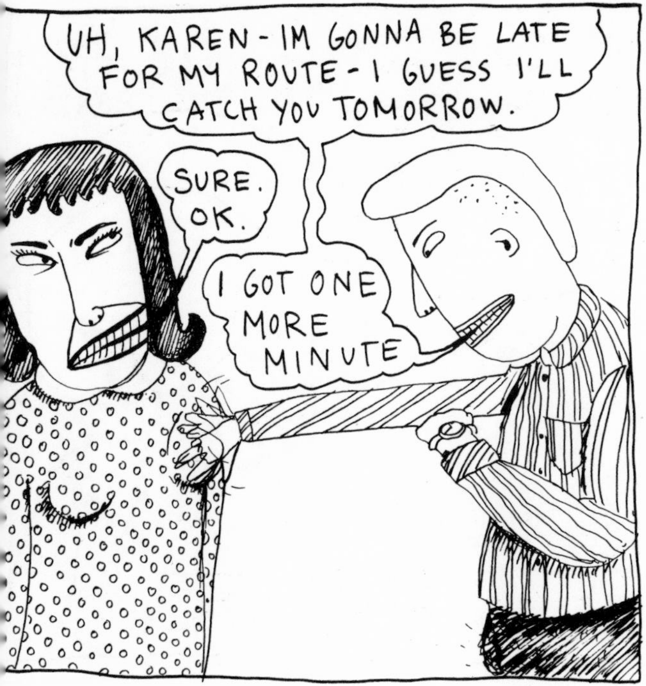
UH, KAREN - IM GONNA BE LATE FOR MY ROUTE - I GUESS I'LL CATCH YOU TOMORROW.
SURE. OK.
I GOT ONE MORE MINUTE

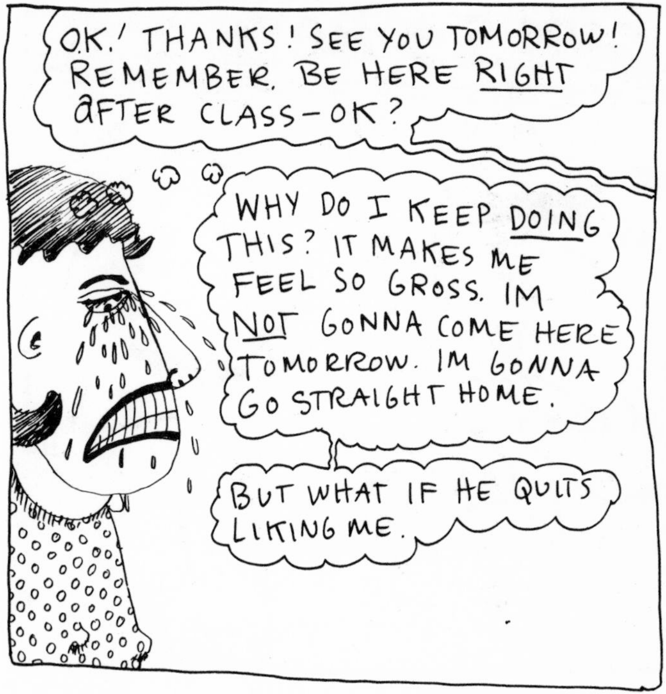
O.K.! THANKS! SEE YOU TOMORROW! REMEMBER. BE HERE RIGHT AFTER CLASS - OK?
WHY DO I KEEP DOING THIS? IT MAKES ME FEEL SO GROSS. IM NOT GONNA COME HERE TOMORROW. IM GONNA GO STRAIGHT HOME.
BUT WHAT IF HE QUITS LIKING ME.

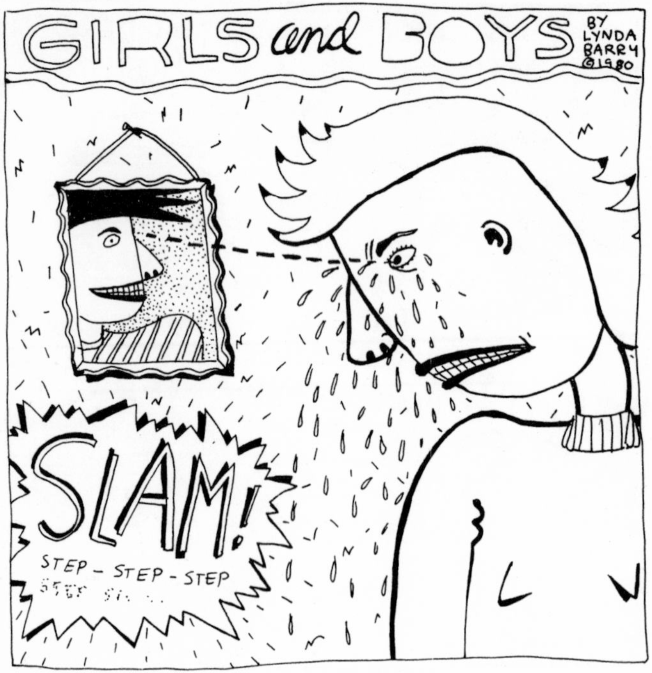
GIRLS and BOYS
BY LYNDA BARRY ©1980
SLAM!
STEP - STEP - STEP

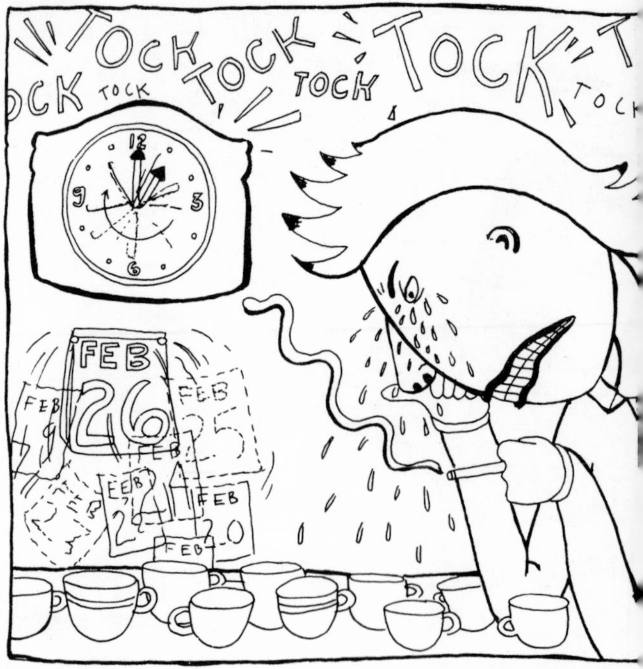
OCK TOCK TOCK TOCK TOCK TOCK TOCK TOCK
12
9
3
6
FEB 26
FEB 25
FEB 20

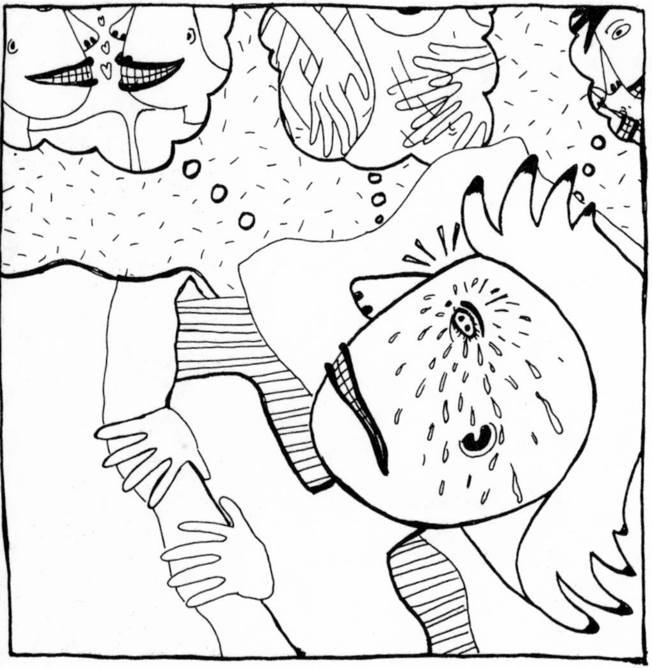

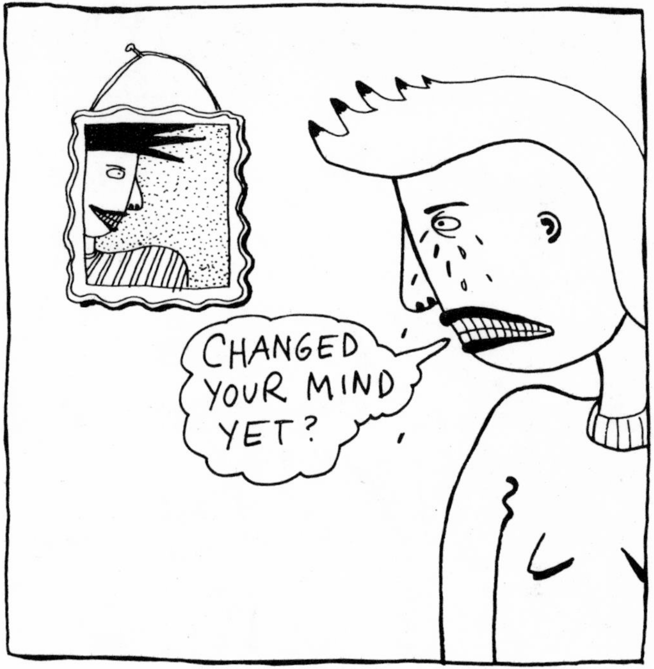
CHANGED YOUR MIND YET?

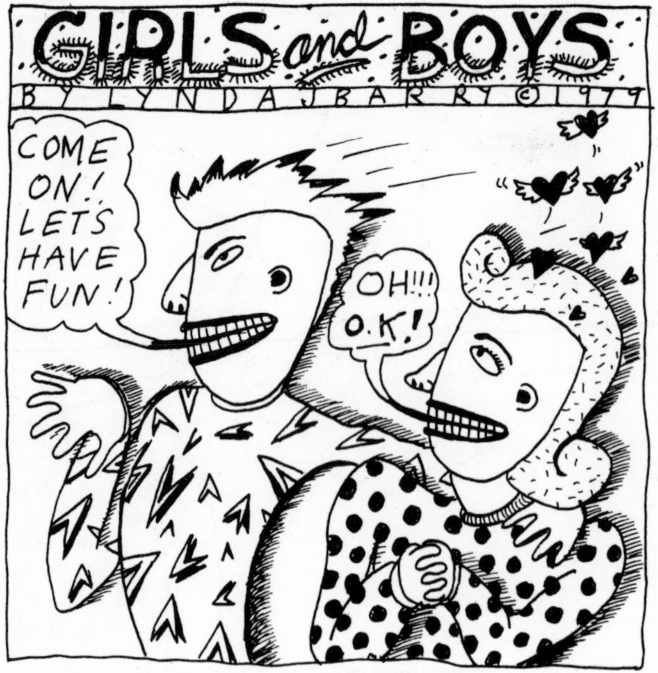
GIRLS and BOYS
BY LYNDA J BARRY ©1979
COME ON! LETS HAVE FUN!
OH!!! O.K.!

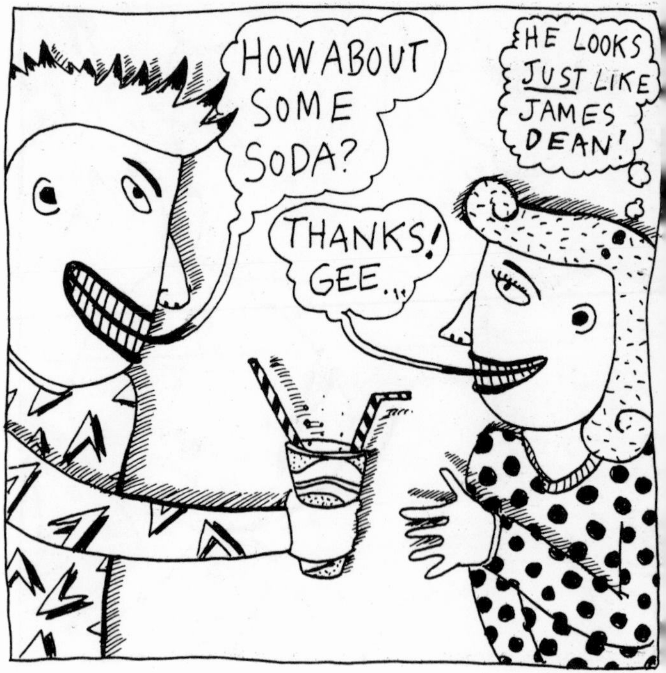
HOW ABOUT SOME SODA?
HE LOOKS JUST LIKE JAMES DEAN!
THANKS! GEE...

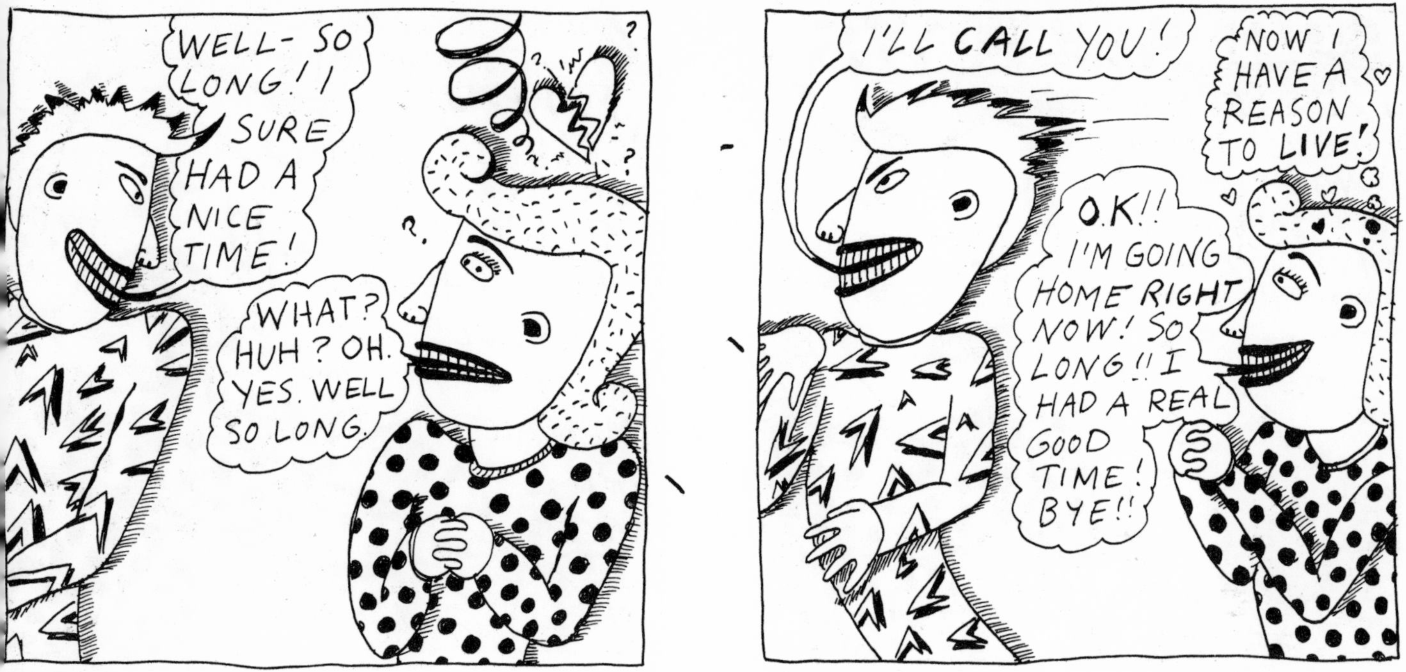
WELL- SO LONG!! I SURE HAD A NICE TIME!
WHAT? HUH? OH. YES. WELL SO LONG.
I'LL CALL YOU!
O.K!! I'M GOING HOME RIGHT NOW! SO LONG!! I HAD A REAL GOOD TIME! BYE!!
NOW I HAVE A REASON TO LIVE!

continued

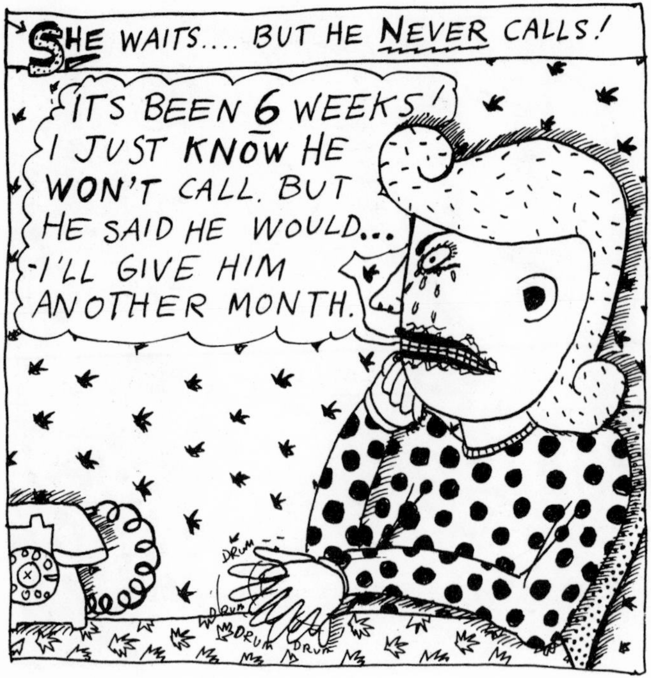
SHE WAITS.... BUT HE NEVER CALLS!
IT'S BEEN 6 WEEKS! I JUST KNOW HE WON'T CALL. BUT HE SAID HE WOULD... -I'LL GIVE HIM ANOTHER MONTH.
DRUM
DRUM
DRUM
DRUM

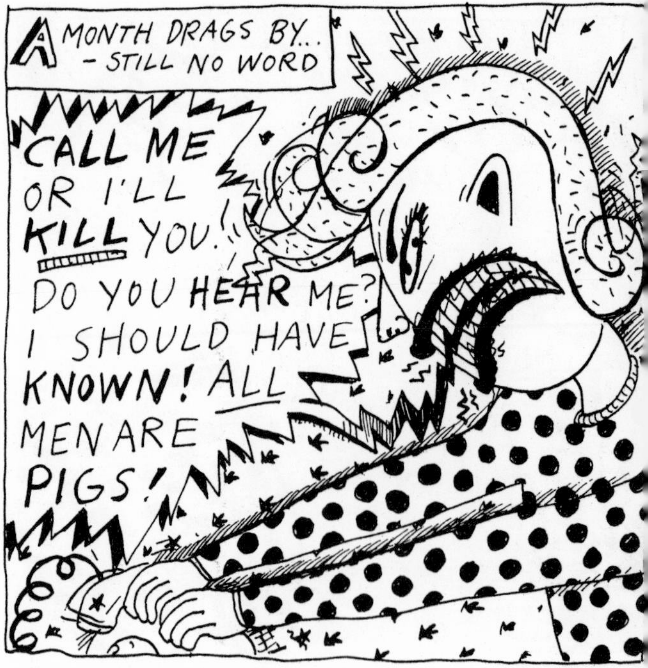
A MONTH DRAGS BY... - STILL NO WORD
CALL ME OR I'LL KILL YOU. DO YOU HEAR ME? I SHOULD HAVE KNOWN! ALL MEN ARE PIGS!

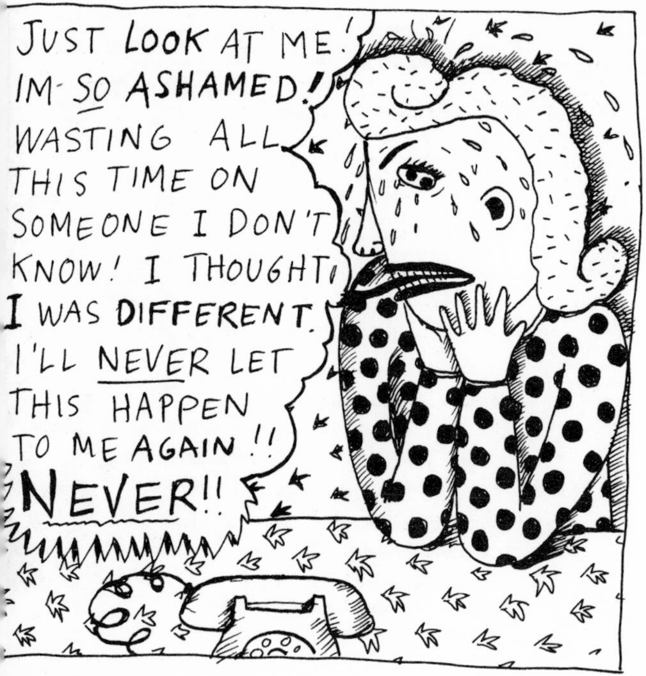
JUST LOOK AT ME! IM SO ASHAMED! WASTING ALL THIS TIME ON SOMEONE I DON'T KNOW! I THOUGHT I WAS DIFFERENT. I'LL NEVER LET THIS HAPPEN TO ME AGAIN!! NEVER!!

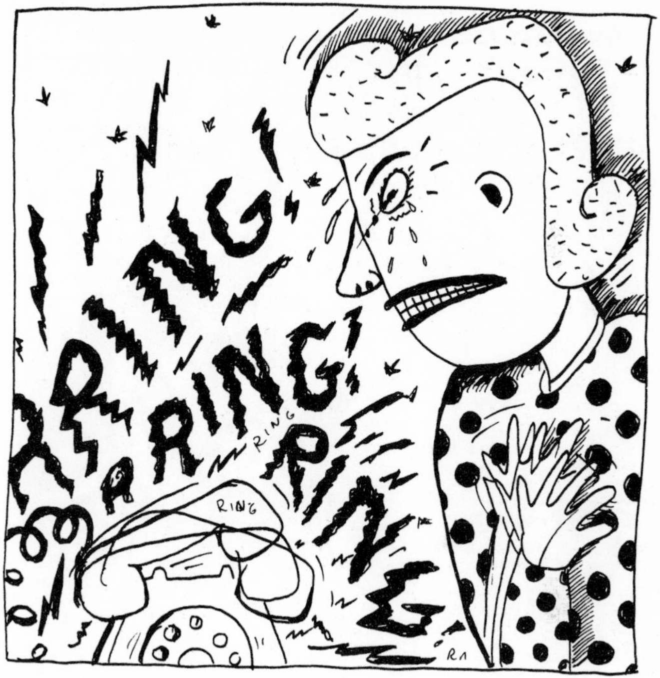
RING! RING! RING!
RING
RING

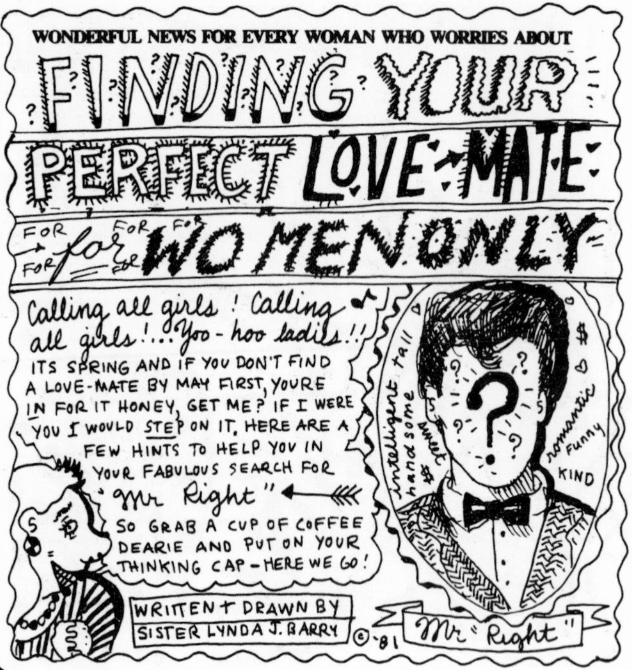

WONDERFUL NEWS FOR EVERY WOMAN WHO WORRIES ABOUT
FINDING YOUR PERFECT LOVE-MATE
FOR FOR FOR FOR for FOR WOMEN ONLY
Calling all girls! Calling all girls!... Yoo-hoo ladies!!
ITS SPRING AND IF YOU DON'T FIND A LOVE-MATE BY MAY FIRST, YOURE IN FOR IT HONEY, GET ME? IF I WERE YOU I WOULD STEP ON IT. HERE ARE A FEW HINTS TO HELP YOU IN YOUR FABULOUS SEARCH FOR "Mr Right"
SO GRAB A CUP OF COFFEE DEARIE AND PUT ON YOUR THINKING CAP - HERE WE GO!
intelligent tall handsome
romantic
Funny
KIND
WRITTEN + DRAWN BY SISTER LYNDA J. BARRY
© '81
Mr "Right"

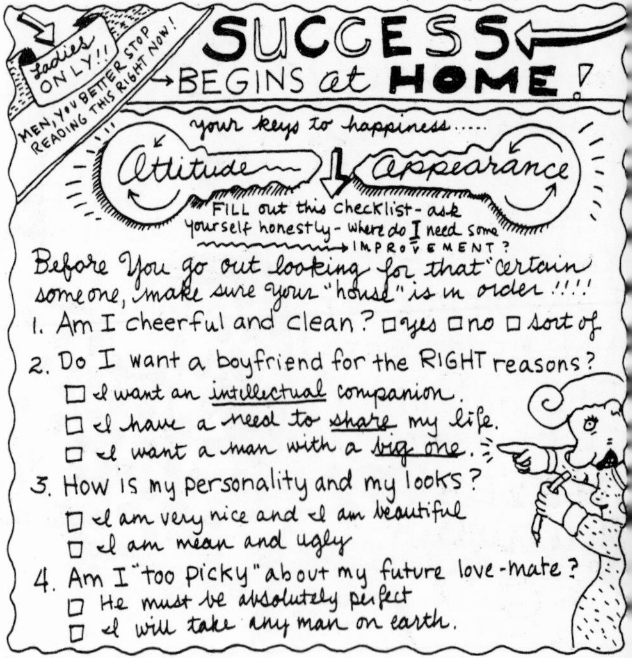

Ladies ONLY!!
MEN YOU BETTER STOP READING THIS RIGHT NOW!
SUCCESS BEGINS at HOME!
your keys to happiness.....
Attitude
appearance
FILL out this checklist - ask yourself honestly - where do I need some IMPROVEMENT?
Before You go out looking for that "certain someone, make sure your "house" is in order!!!!
1. Am I cheerful and clean? □ yes □ no □ sort of
2. Do I want a boyfriend for the RIGHT reasons?
□ I want an intellectual companion.
□ I have a need to share my life.
□ I want a man with a big one.
3. How is my personality and my looks?
□ I am very nice and I am beautiful
□ I am mean and ugly
4. Am I "too picky" about my future love-mate?
□ He must be absolutely perfect
□ I will take any man on earth.

JUST WHO IS Mr Right?

Just what are you looking for in a man? Never mind what others find attractive... what is it that YOU desire. Here is a helpful list to help you define your goals. Check the qualities you feel are important

LOOKS

- ☐ he MUST BE very handsome
- ☐ he must be unusually cute
- ☐ he must not frighten children

BRAINS

- ☐ he MUST Be a genius
- ☐ he must be able to read
- ☐ he must have a big one

Sense of Humor

ha ha ha

- ☐ he must think my jokes are the funniest ones in the world
- ☐ he cannot laugh at me
- ☐ It is ok. if he laughs at others but not to be mean

Penis Size

- ☐ "I don't really look out for penis size, but I notice it"
- ☐ Penis size doesn't matter
- ☐ I want a man with a monster

$MONEY?$

- ☐ He must be Solvent
- ☐ He must be rich
- ☐ Penis size doesn't matter

JOB

- ☐ Must have one
- ☐ Must have one
- ☐ must have one
- ☐ Must have big one

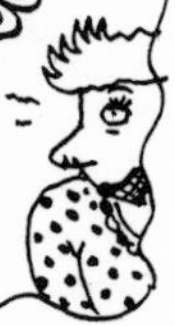

What do I do once I SPOT HIM

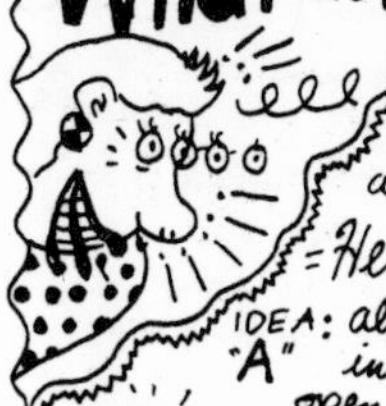

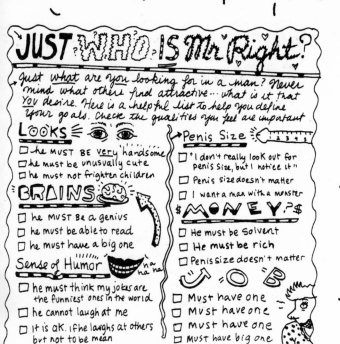

Calm down girl. Be cool. Casual. There he is, across the room. At a party, a bar, a cafe, a check out line. THERE HE IS!!!!!

Here are a few TIPS 'N' TRICKS

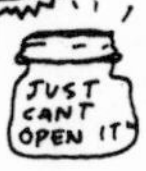
JUST CANT OPEN IT

IDEA "A": always carry a jar with that "too tight" lid in your purse. Take it out and struggle to open it. MAKE SURE YOU FAIL. Walk over to him "nervously" and ask if he would be kind enough to give you "a hand" afterwards, thank him and ask him if he would "take off his pants"

IDEA "B": Shoot a spitwad at him. --- when one "hits," wink and say "Gee. Im sorry. You can "shoot one" at "me" if you'd like to." (This one always gets 'em.)

IDEA "C": Stare at him and smile. Act real "embarassed" when he "catches" you. **Offer money. Try to look french.**

IDEA "D": Be yourself. Act natural. Let him do the work. If he leaves without speaking to you, follow him to his car and sit on the hood. **Let him notice you.**

IDEA "E": Go over to him and ask politely "Is this seat taken?" then point to his lap.

What shall we talk ABOUT

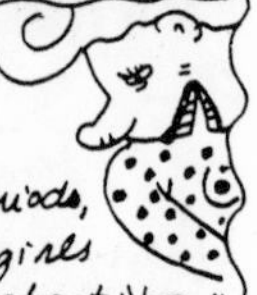

Once you've "broken the ice" you want to make "sure" not to "blow it." Alot of women go "wrong" right after they meet a fellow by wanting to talk about doing their hair, their periods, their complexion problems. NIX, gals!! Other girls try to "pal" around with Mr Right by talking about "boy" topics, like salami, trains, cigars, the spaceneedle. No-No, sweets. Lissen up. Remember:

1. **Let him** pick the conversational topic. Try to figure out just what you think he'll say then timidly say it first - as if you "arent sure"
2. Stare at him while he talks. When you talk look at your hands, embarassed. Interrupt him to feel his muscle. If you have to p, hold it.
3. If he is smart you might try to "impress" him by being smart also. If he is dumb keep feeling his muscles

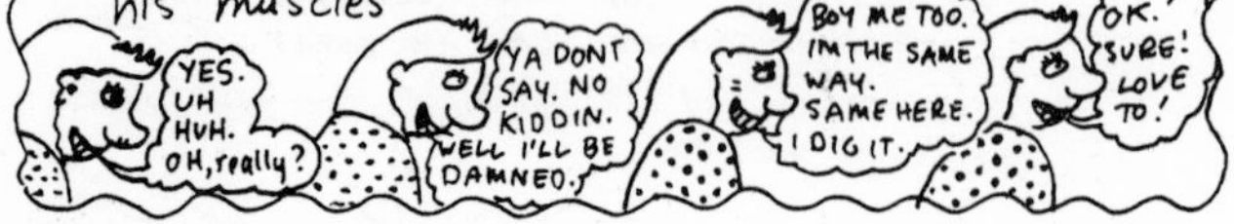
YES. UH HUH. OH, really?
YA DONT SAY. NO KIDDIN. WELL I'LL BE DAMNED.
BOY ME TOO. IM THE SAME WAY. SAME HERE. I DIG IT.
OK! SURE! LOVE TO!

What shall we do on OUR 1st DATE

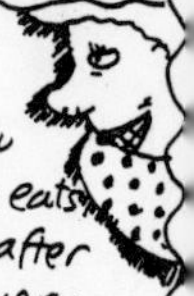

EATING together

is an absolute must!!!! It is said that you can tell what sort of lover a man is by how he eats. Like if he eats real fast then falls asleep right after maybe you better go home. Or if he eats very very slowly and moans each time he puts something in his mouth and talks about what nice food it is and afterwards he pulls the plate gently toward him and strokes its hair and whispers oh baby. Or he might be scared to try different foods. Or he just eats what he wants and leaves the rest unfinished and then picks his teeth and says "gotta go." Maybe he wants to eat only with the lights out or he has to call the food "Mommy"

SO you better go out to eat together. And if you cant, - bring a doughnut in your purse and ask him could he please eat it for you.

Does he like:

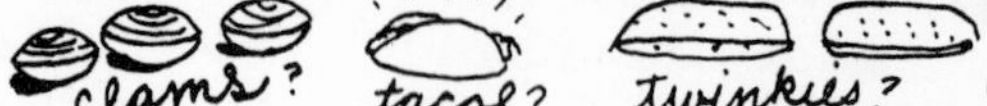

clams? tacos? twinkies?

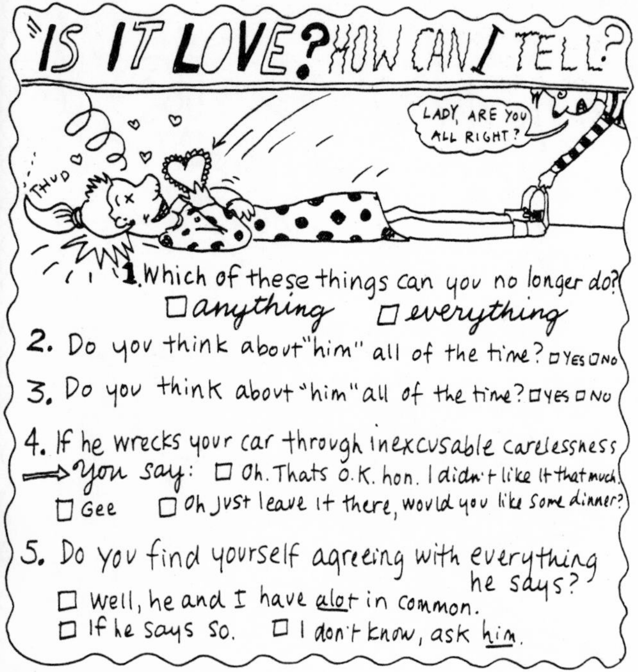
IS IT LOVE? HOW CAN I TELL?
LADY, ARE YOU ALL RIGHT?
THUD
1. Which of these things can you no longer do?
☐ anything ☐ everything
2. Do you think about "him" all of the time? ☐ Yes ☐ No
3. Do you think about "him" all of the time? ☐ YES ☐ NO
4. If he wrecks your car through inexcusable carelessness
→ You say: ☐ Oh. Thats O.K. hon. I didn't like It that much.
☐ Gee ☐ Oh just leave it there, would you like some dinner?
5. Do you find yourself agreeing with everything he says?
☐ Well, he and I have alot in common.
☐ If he says so. ☐ I don't know, ask him.

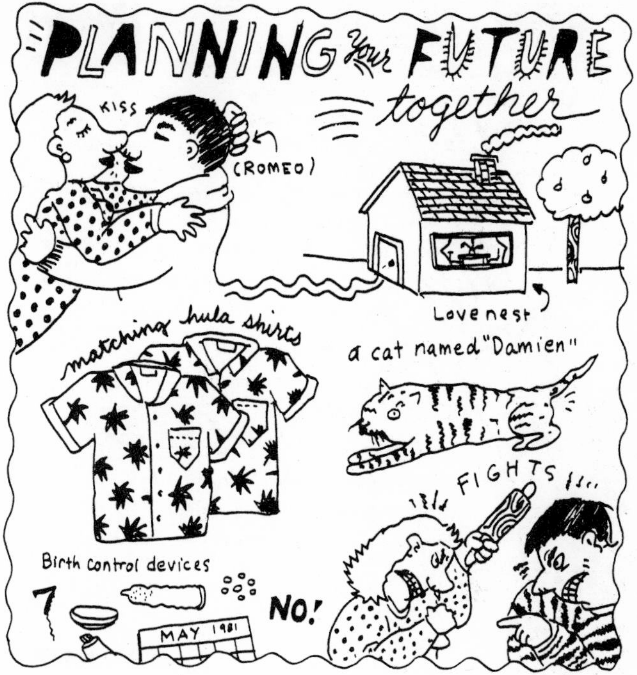
PLANNING your FUTURE together
KISS
(ROMEO)
Love nest
matching hula shirts
a cat named "Damien"
FIGHTS
Birth control devices
7
MAY 1981
NO!

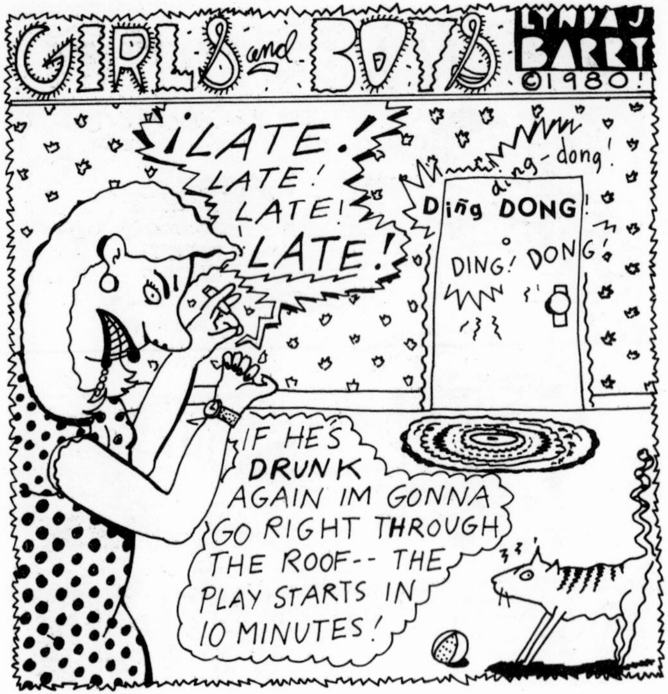
GIRLS and BOYS
LYNDA J BARRY ©1980!
¡LATE!
LATE! LATE! LATE!
ding-dong!
Ding DONG
DING! DONG!
IF HE'S DRUNK AGAIN IM GONNA GO RIGHT THROUGH THE ROOF-- THE PLAY STARTS IN 10 MINUTES!

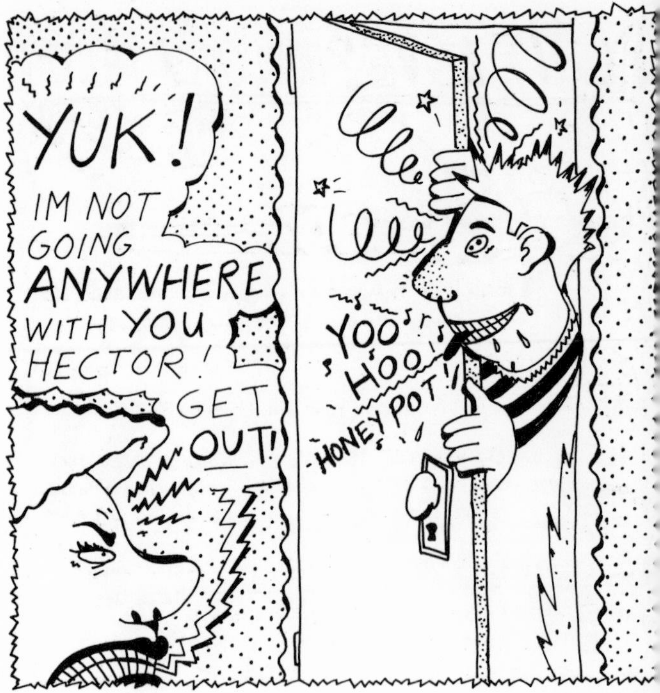
YUK!
IM NOT GOING ANYWHERE WITH YOU HECTOR!
GET OUT!
YOO HOO HONEY POT!

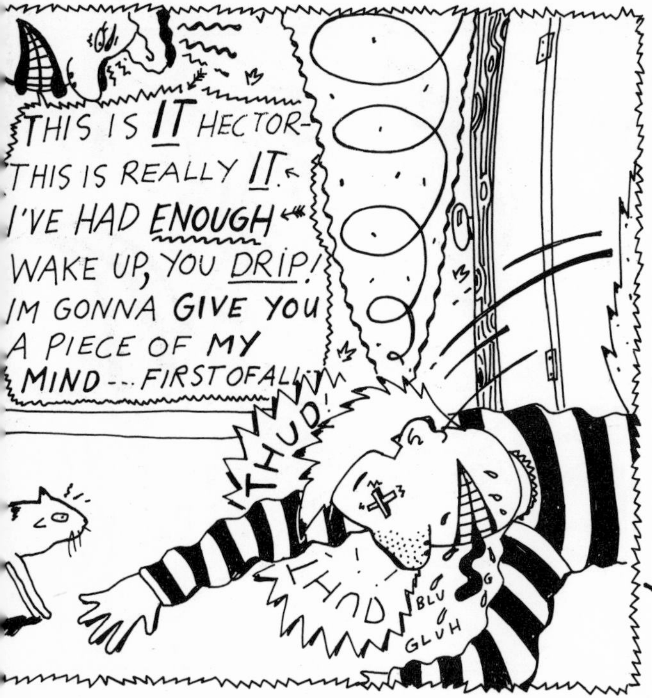
THIS IS IT HECTOR-
THIS IS REALLY IT.
I'VE HAD ENOUGH
WAKE UP, YOU DRIP!
IM GONNA GIVE YOU
A PIECE OF MY
MIND--FIRSTOFALL
THUD!
THUD
BLU
GLUH

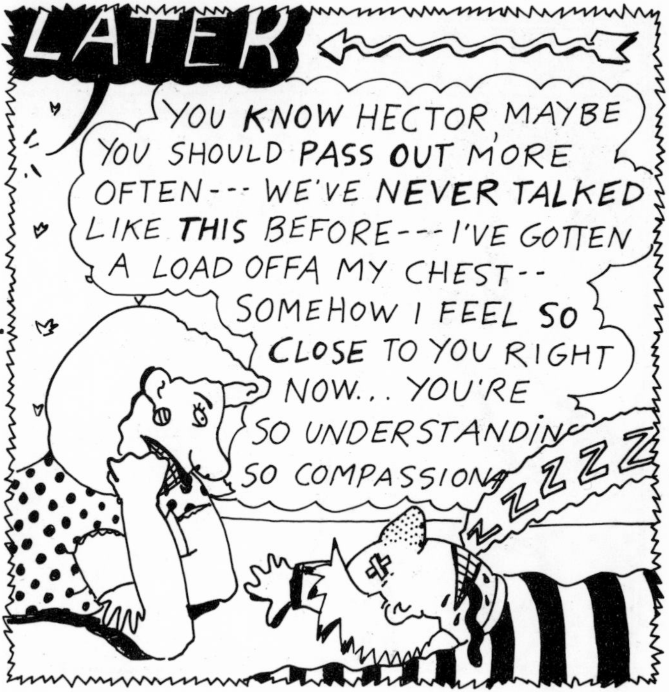
LATER
YOU KNOW HECTOR, MAYBE YOU SHOULD PASS OUT MORE OFTEN--- WE'VE NEVER TALKED LIKE THIS BEFORE---I'VE GOTTEN A LOAD OFFA MY CHEST-- SOMEHOW I FEEL SO CLOSE TO YOU RIGHT NOW... YOU'RE SO UNDERSTANDIN SO COMPASSION
ZZZZZZ

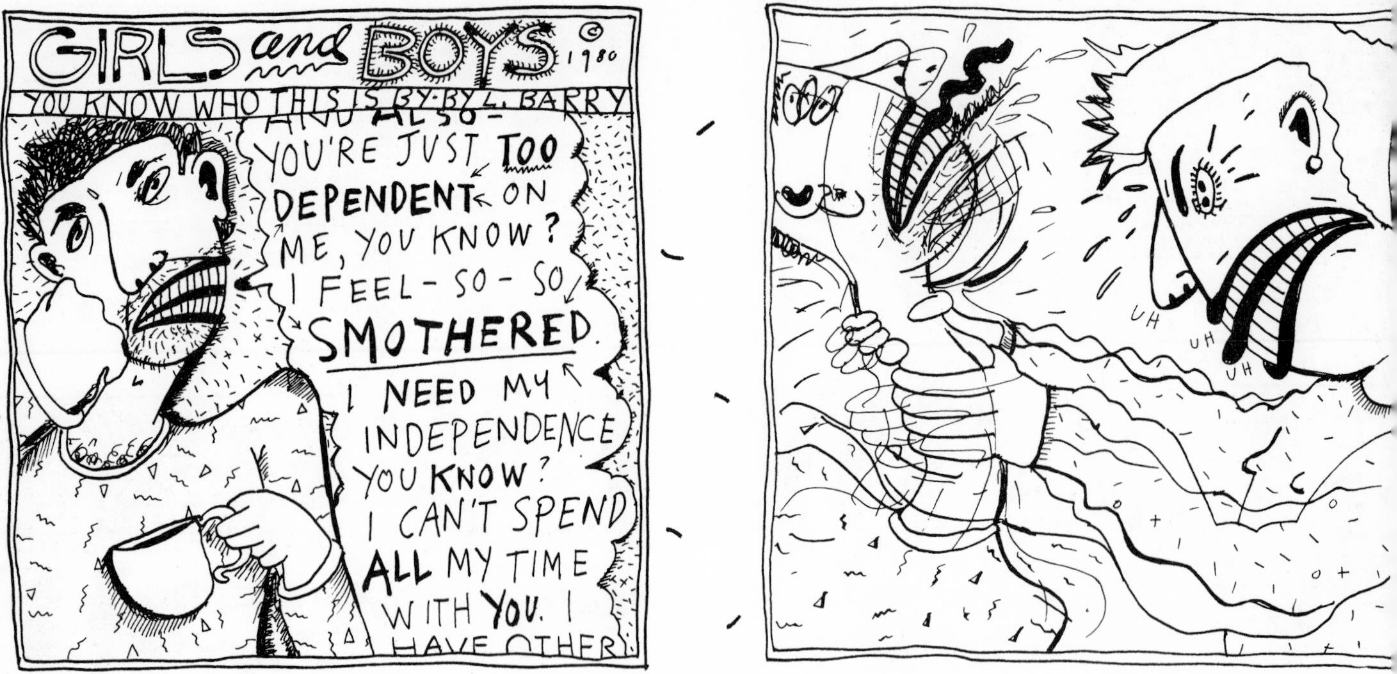
GIRLS and BOYS © 1980
YOU KNOW WHO THIS IS BY·BY L. BARRY
AND ALSO - YOU'RE JUST TOO DEPENDENT ON ME, YOU KNOW? I FEEL- SO - SO SMOTHERED. I NEED MY INDEPENDENCE YOU KNOW? I CAN'T SPEND ALL MY TIME WITH YOU. I HAVE OTHER
UH
UH
UH

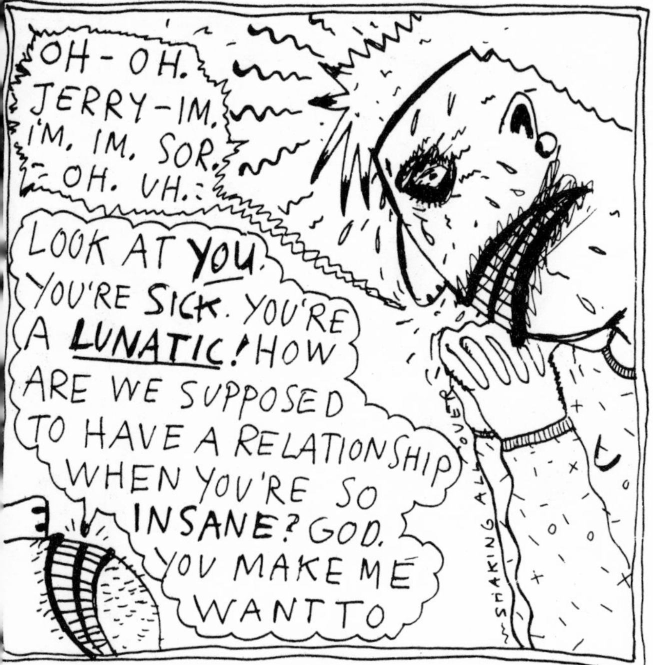
OH-OH. JERRY-IM. IM. IM. SOR. OH. UH.
LOOK AT YOU. YOU'RE SICK. YOU'RE A LUNATIC! HOW ARE WE SUPPOSED TO HAVE A RELATIONSHIP WHEN YOU'RE SO INSANE? GOD. YOU MAKE ME WANT TO
SHAKING ALL OVER

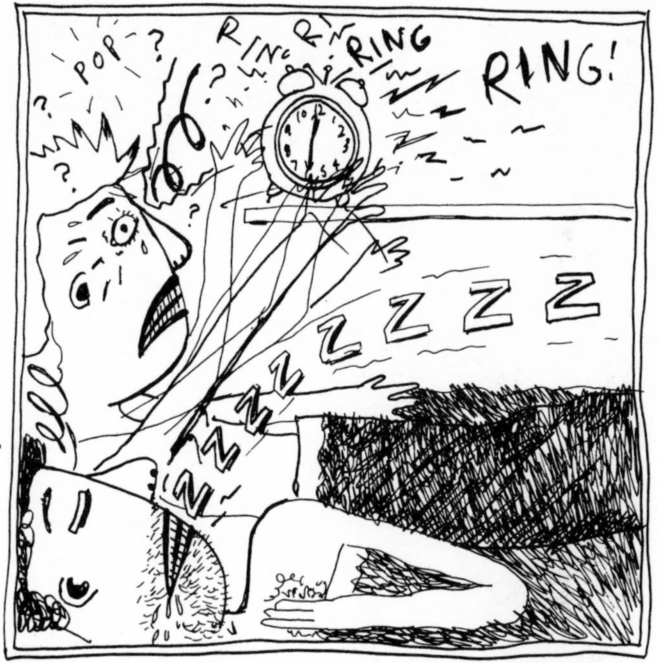
POP
RING
RING!
ZZZZZ

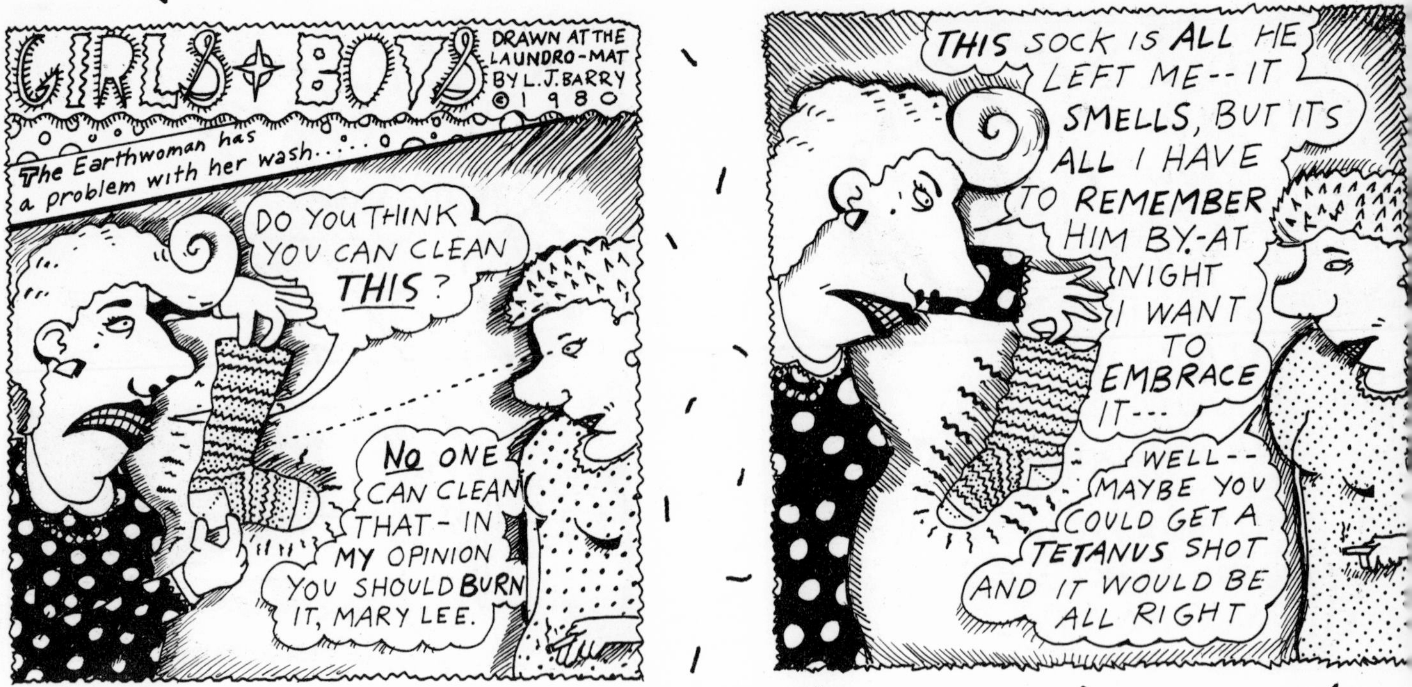

GIRLS + BOYS
DRAWN AT THE LAUNDRO-MAT BY L.J. BARRY ©1980
The Earthwoman has a problem with her wash.....
DO YOU THINK YOU CAN CLEAN THIS?
NO ONE CAN CLEAN THAT - IN MY OPINION YOU SHOULD BURN IT, MARY LEE.
THIS SOCK IS ALL HE LEFT ME-- IT SMELLS, BUT ITS ALL I HAVE TO REMEMBER HIM BY.-AT NIGHT I WANT TO EMBRACE IT---
WELL-- MAYBE YOU COULD GET A TETANUS SHOT AND IT WOULD BE ALL RIGHT

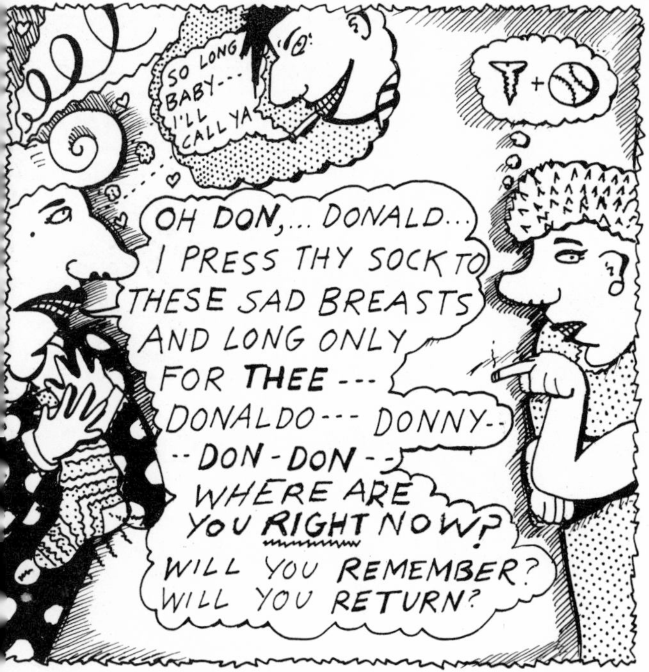
SO LONG BABY--- I'LL CALLYA
OH DON,... DONALD... I PRESS THY SOCK TO THESE SAD BREASTS AND LONG ONLY FOR THEE--- DONALDO--- DONNY-- --DON-DON-- WHERE ARE YOU RIGHT NOW? WILL YOU REMEMBER? WILL YOU RETURN?

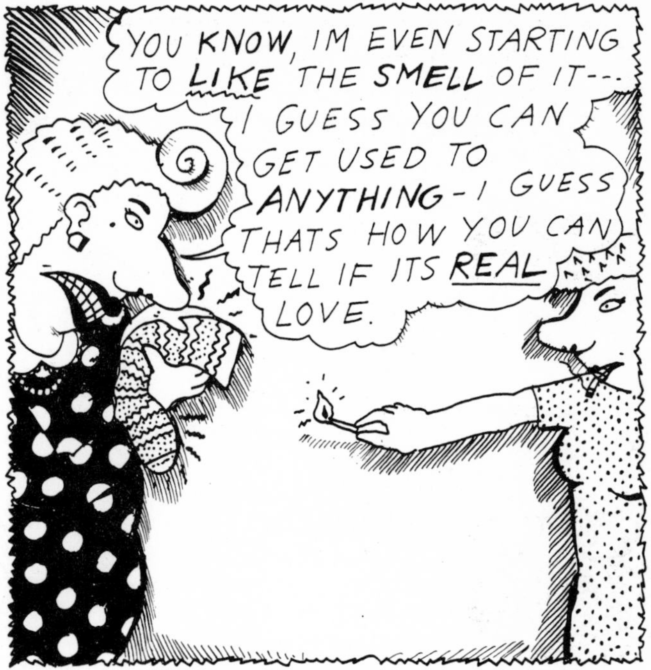
YOU KNOW, IM EVEN STARTING TO LIKE THE SMELL OF IT--- I GUESS YOU CAN GET USED TO ANYTHING - I GUESS THATS HOW YOU CAN TELL IF ITS REAL LOVE.

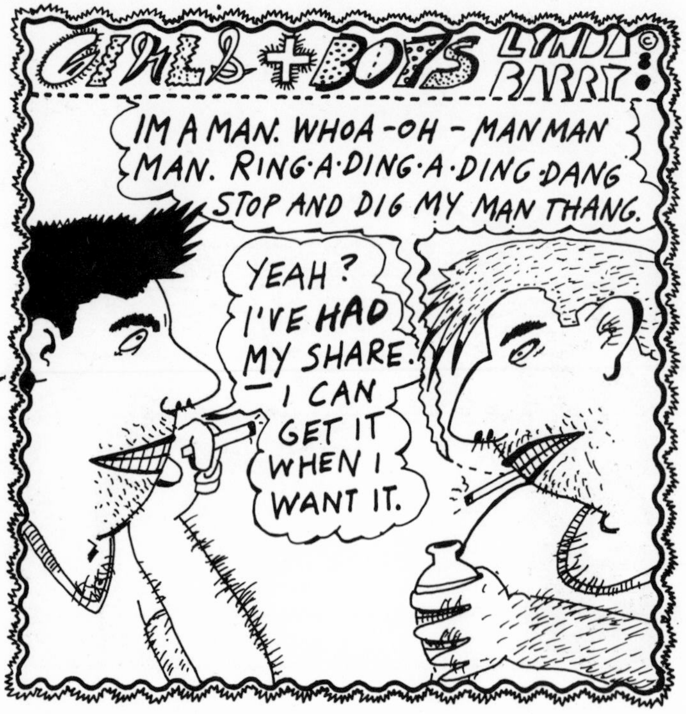
GIRLS + BOYS
LYNDA BARRY ©
IM A MAN. WHOA-OH - MAN MAN MAN. RING·A·DING·A·DING·DANG STOP AND DIG MY MAN THANG.
YEAH? I'VE HAD MY SHARE. — I CAN GET IT WHEN I WANT IT.

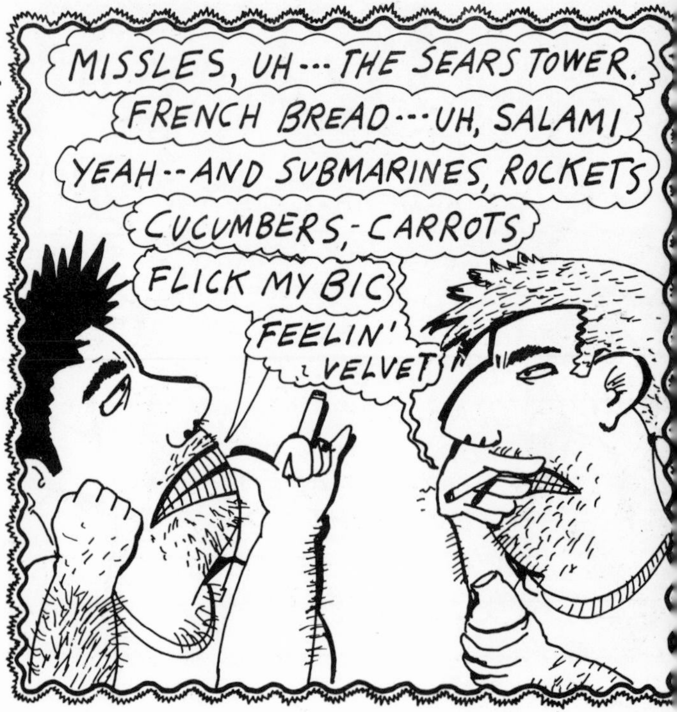
MISSLES, UH --- THE SEARS TOWER.
FRENCH BREAD --- UH, SALAMI
YEAH -- AND SUBMARINES, ROCKETS
CUCUMBERS, - CARROTS
FLICK MY BIC
FEELIN' VELVET

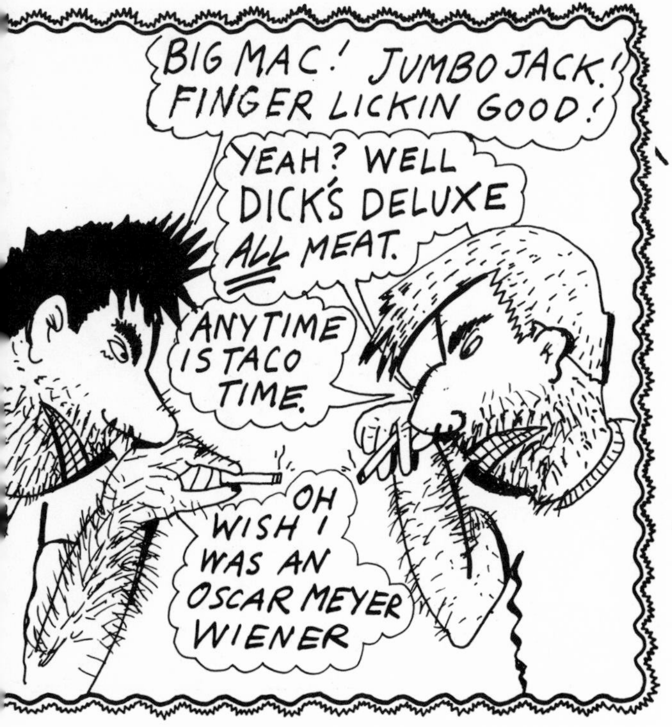
BIG MAC! JUMBO JACK! FINGER LICKIN GOOD!
YEAH? WELL DICK'S DELUXE ALL MEAT.
ANYTIME IS TACO TIME.
OH WISH I WAS AN OSCAR MEYER WIENER

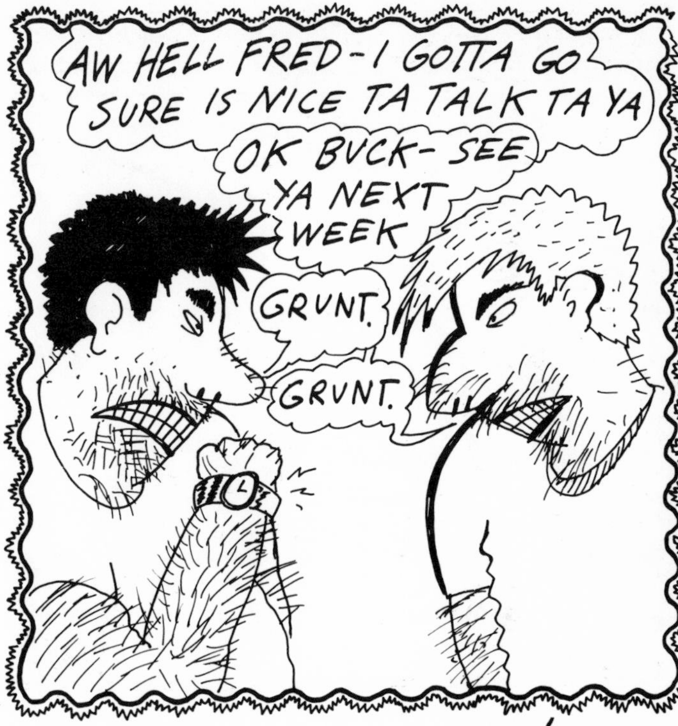
AW HELL FRED - I GOTTA GO SURE IS NICE TA TALK TA YA
OK BUCK - SEE YA NEXT WEEK
GRUNT.
GRUNT.

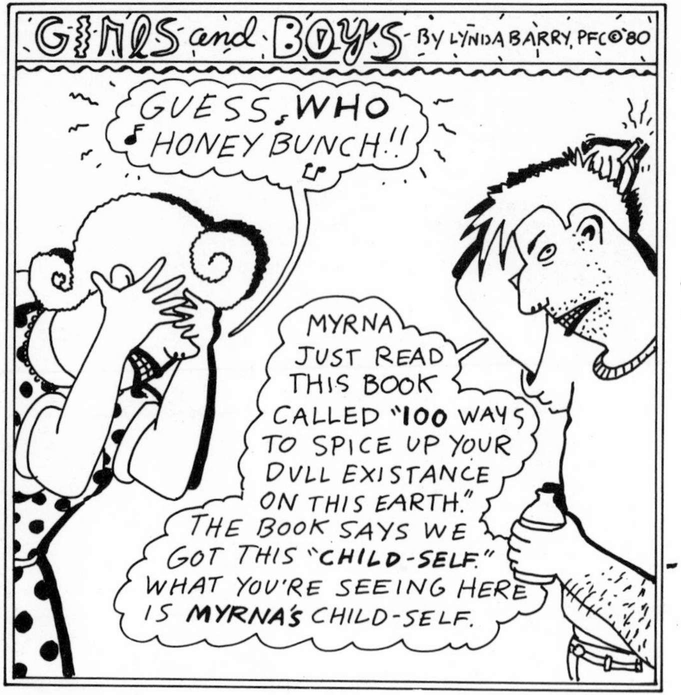
GIRLS and BOYS BY LYNDA BARRY, PFC©'80
GUESS WHO HONEY BUNCH!!
MYRNA JUST READ THIS BOOK CALLED "100 WAYS TO SPICE UP YOUR DULL EXISTANCE ON THIS EARTH." THE BOOK SAYS WE GOT THIS "CHILD-SELF." WHAT YOU'RE SEEING HERE IS MYRNA'S CHILD-SELF.

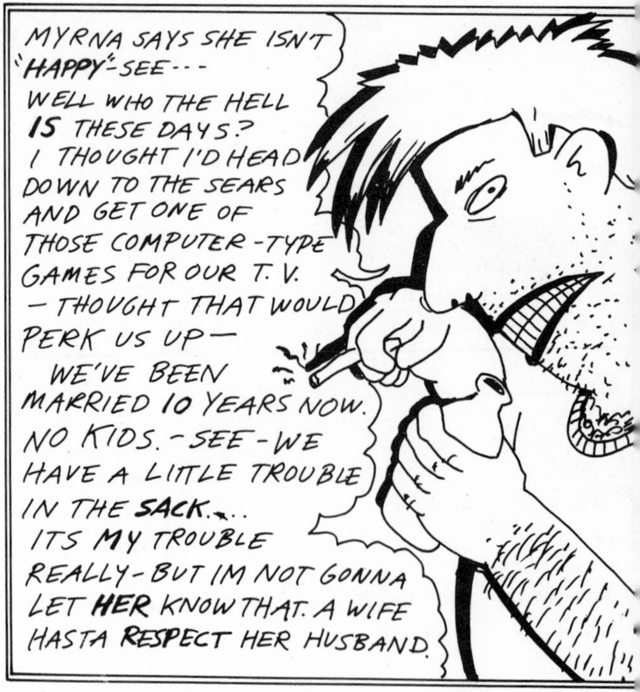
MYRNA SAYS SHE ISN'T "HAPPY"-SEE--- WELL WHO THE HELL IS THESE DAYS? I THOUGHT I'D HEAD DOWN TO THE SEARS AND GET ONE OF THOSE COMPUTER-TYPE GAMES FOR OUR T.V. - THOUGHT THAT WOULD PERK US UP- WE'VE BEEN MARRIED 10 YEARS NOW. NO KIDS. - SEE - WE HAVE A LITTLE TROUBLE IN THE SACK... ITS MY TROUBLE REALLY - BUT IM NOT GONNA LET HER KNOW THAT. A WIFE HASTA RESPECT HER HUSBAND.

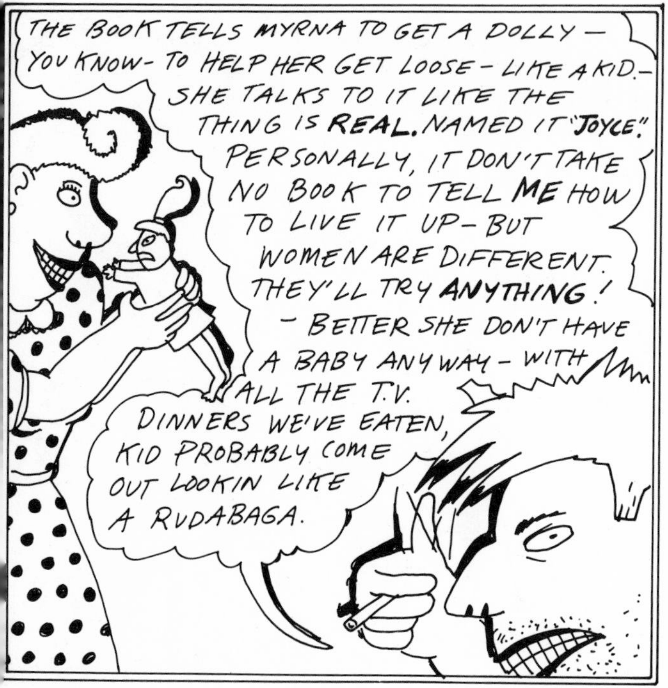
THE BOOK TELLS MYRNA TO GET A DOLLY — YOU KNOW — TO HELP HER GET LOOSE — LIKE A KID. — SHE TALKS TO IT LIKE THE THING IS **REAL.** NAMED IT "JOYCE." PERSONALLY, IT DON'T TAKE NO BOOK TO TELL **ME** HOW TO LIVE IT UP — BUT WOMEN ARE DIFFERENT. THEY'LL TRY **ANYTHING**! — BETTER SHE DON'T HAVE A BABY ANYWAY — WITH ALL THE T.V. DINNERS WE'VE EATEN, KID PROBABLY COME OUT LOOKIN LIKE A RUDABAGA.

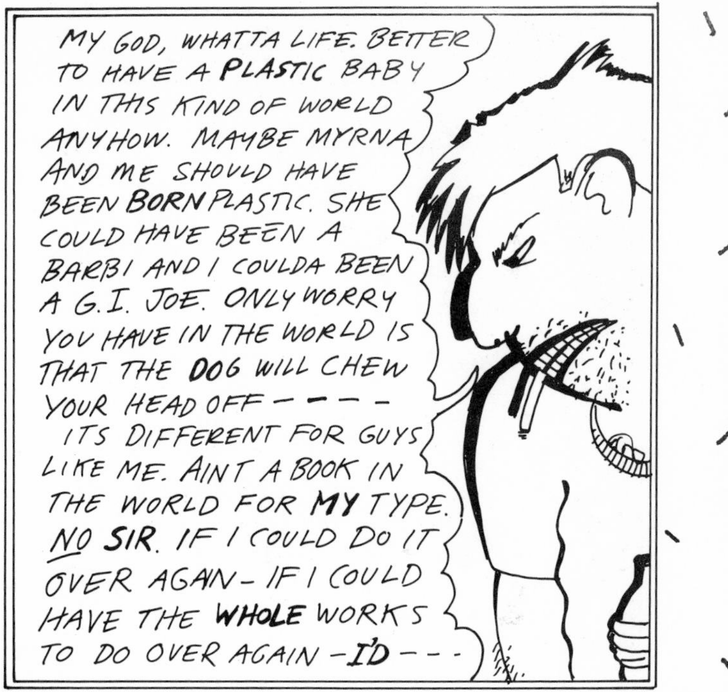
MY GOD, WHATTA LIFE. BETTER TO HAVE A **PLASTIC** BABY IN THIS KIND OF WORLD ANYHOW. MAYBE MYRNA AND ME SHOULD HAVE BEEN **BORN** PLASTIC. SHE COULD HAVE BEEN A BARBI AND I COULDA BEEN A G.I. JOE. ONLY WORRY YOU HAVE IN THE WORLD IS THAT THE **DOG** WILL CHEW YOUR HEAD OFF — — — — ITS DIFFERENT FOR GUYS LIKE ME. AINT A BOOK IN THE WORLD FOR **MY** TYPE. **NO SIR**. IF I COULD DO IT OVER AGAIN — IF I COULD HAVE THE **WHOLE** WORKS TO DO OVER AGAIN — **I'D** — — —

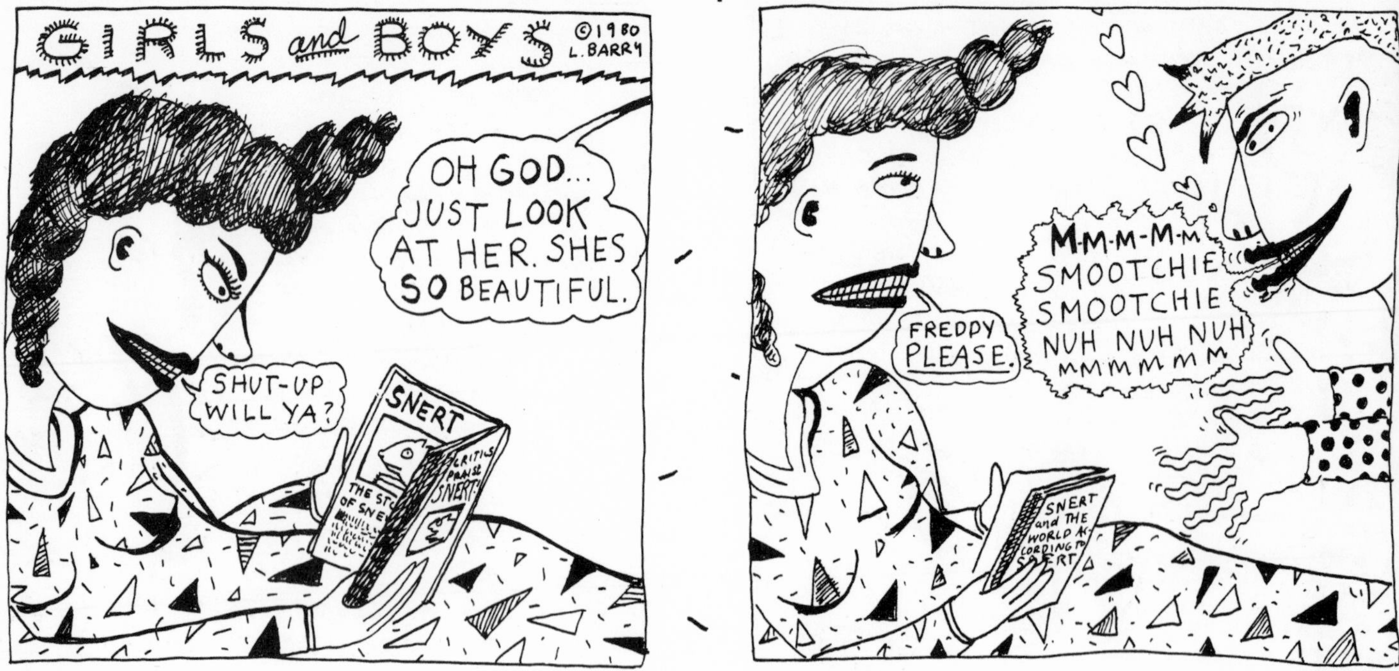
GIRLS and BOYS
©1980 L. BARRY
OH GOD... JUST LOOK AT HER. SHES SO BEAUTIFUL.
SHUT-UP WILL YA?
SNERT
CRITICS PRAISE SNERT!
FREDDY PLEASE.
M-M-M-M-M SMOOTCHIE SMOOTCHIE NUH NUH NUH MMMMMMM
SNERT and THE WORLD ACCORDING TO SNERT

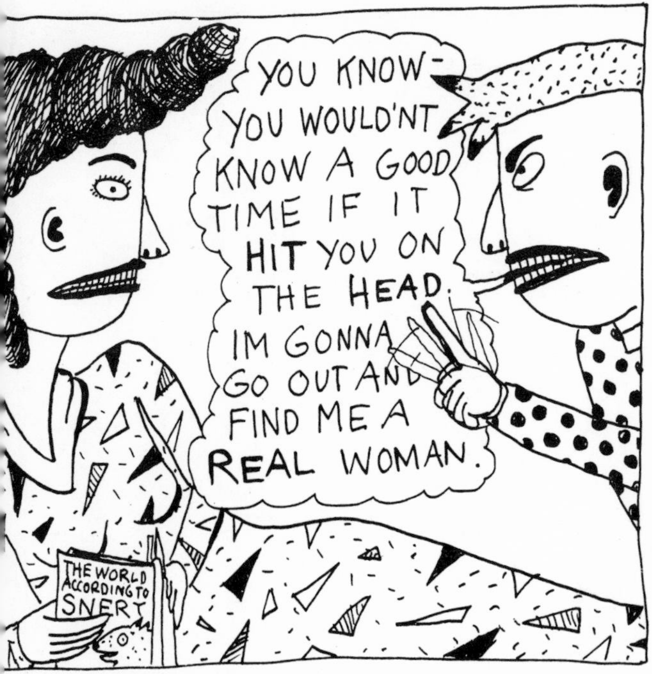
YOU KNOW-
YOU WOULD'NT KNOW A GOOD TIME IF IT HIT YOU ON THE HEAD.
IM GONNA GO OUT AND FIND ME A REAL WOMAN.
THE WORLD ACCORDING TO SNERT

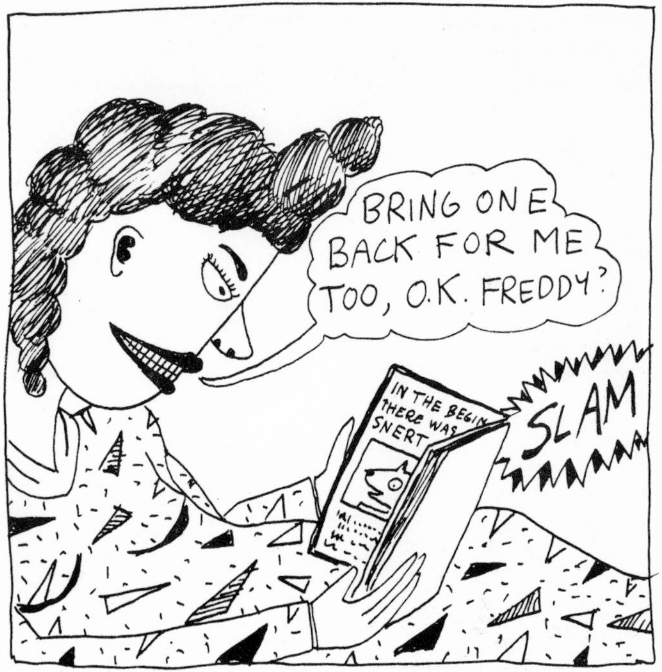
BRING ONE BACK FOR ME TOO, O.K. FREDDY?
IN THE BEGIN THERE WAS SNERT
SLAM

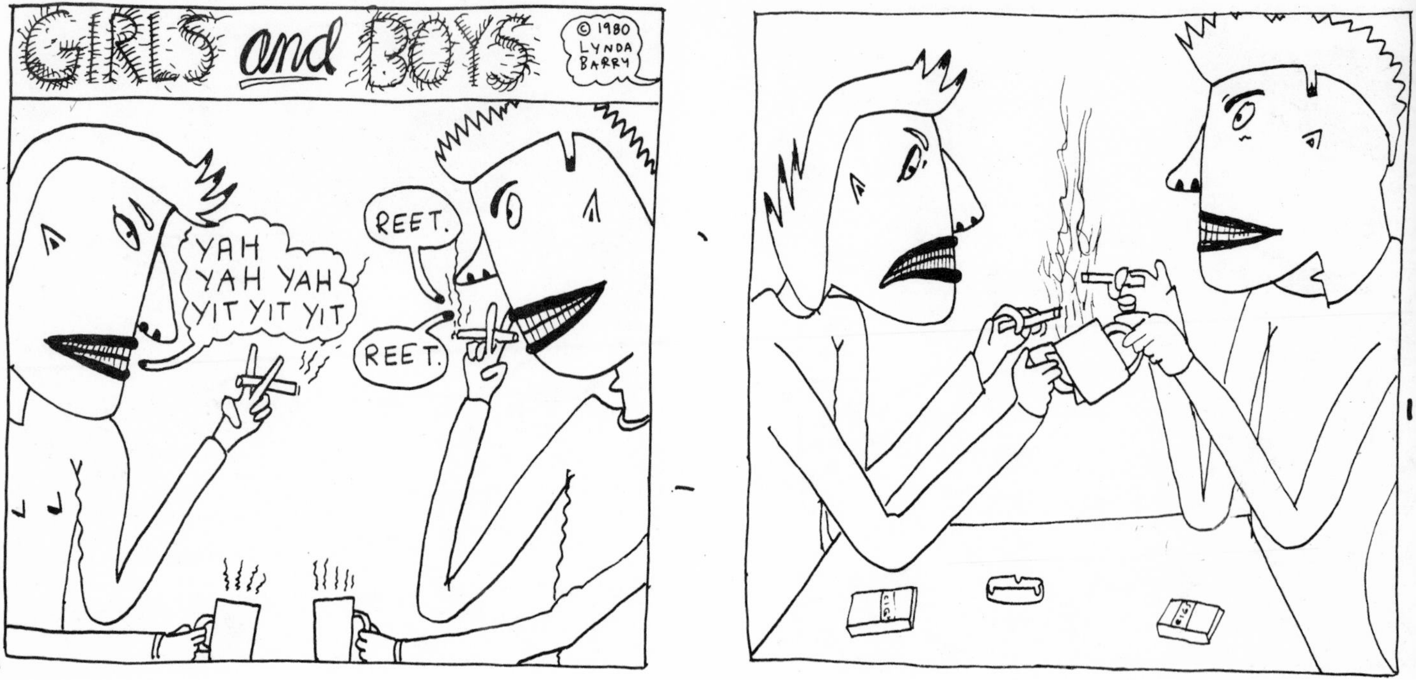
GIRLS and BOYS
© 1980 LYNDA BARRY
YAH YAH YAH YIT YIT YIT
REET.
REET.

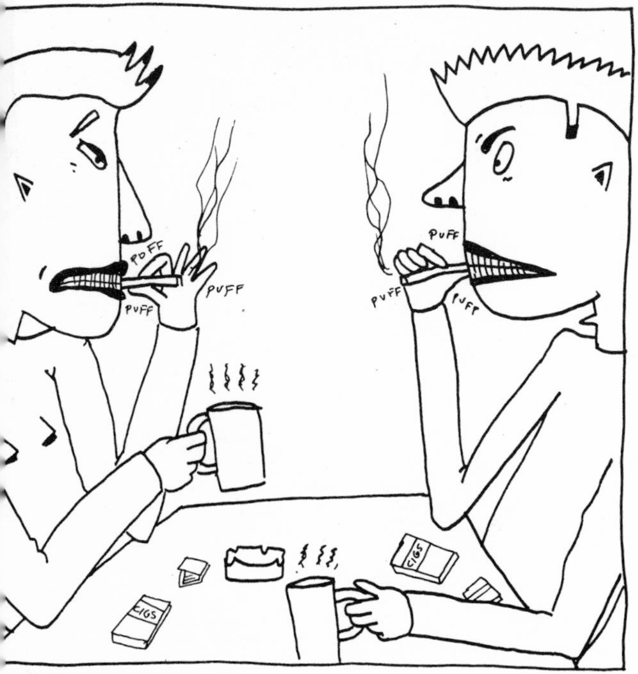
PUFF
PUFF
PUFF
PUFF
PUFF
PUFF
PUFF
CIGS
CIGS

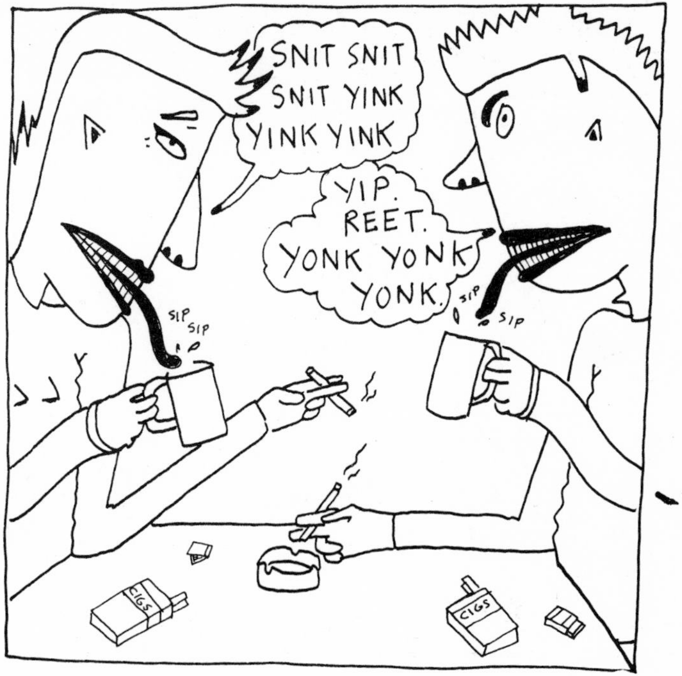
SNIT SNIT SNIT YINK YINK YINK
YIP. REET. YONK YONK YONK YONK.
SIP SIP
SIP
SIP
CIGS
CIGS

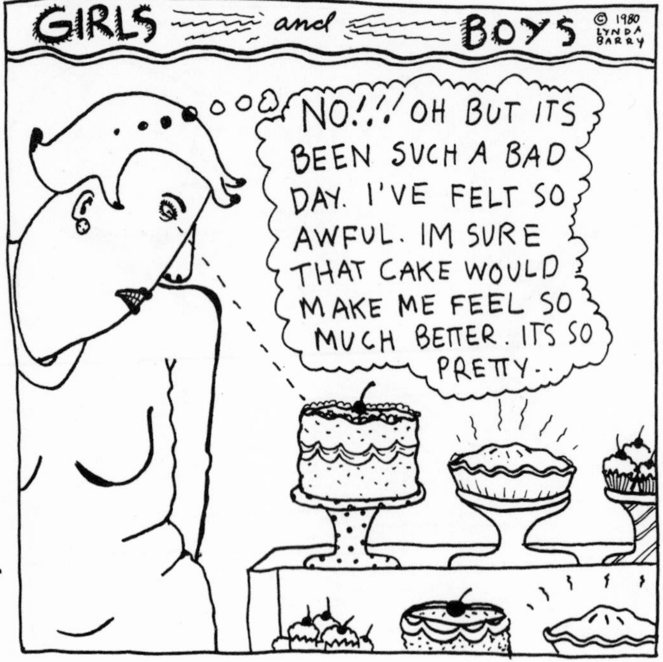
GIRLS and BOYS
© 1980 LYNDA BARRY
NO!!! OH BUT ITS BEEN SUCH A BAD DAY. I'VE FELT SO AWFUL. IM SURE THAT CAKE WOULD MAKE ME FEEL SO MUCH BETTER. ITS SO PRETTY..

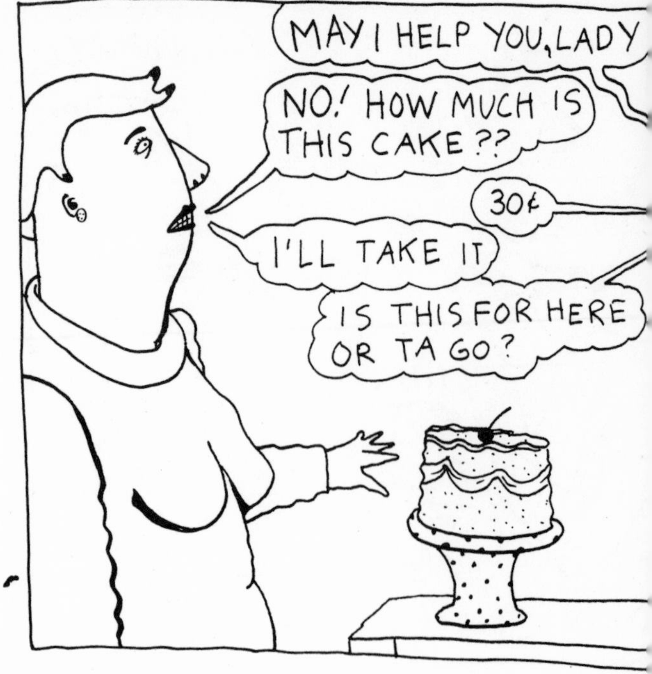
MAY I HELP YOU, LADY
NO! HOW MUCH IS THIS CAKE??
30¢
I'LL TAKE IT
IS THIS FOR HERE OR TA GO?

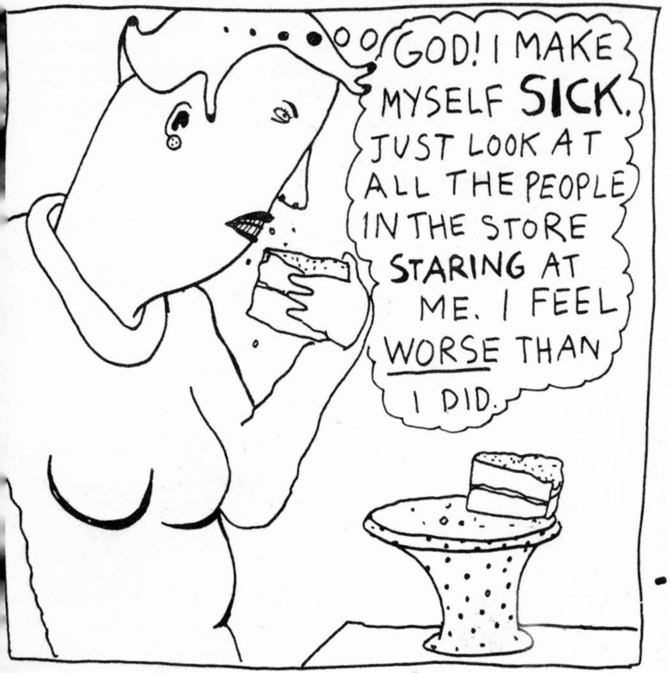
GOD! I MAKE MYSELF SICK. JUST LOOK AT ALL THE PEOPLE IN THE STORE STARING AT ME. I FEEL WORSE THAN I DID.

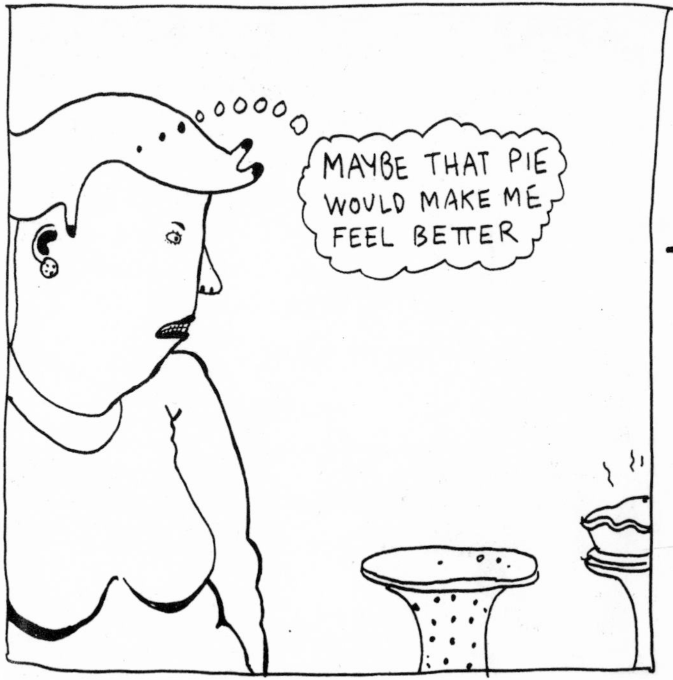
MAYBE THAT PIE WOULD MAKE ME FEEL BETTER

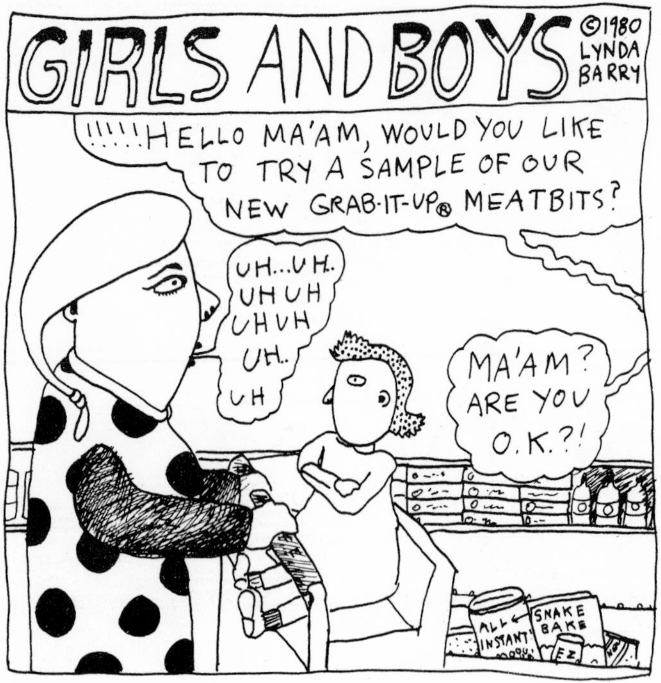
GIRLS AND BOYS
©1980 LYNDA BARRY
!!!!!HELLO MA'AM, WOULD YOU LIKE TO TRY A SAMPLE OF OUR NEW GRAB-IT-UP® MEATBITS?
UH...UH.. UHUH UHUH UH.. UH
MA'AM? ARE YOU O.K.?!
ALL INSTANT
SNAKE BAKE
EZ

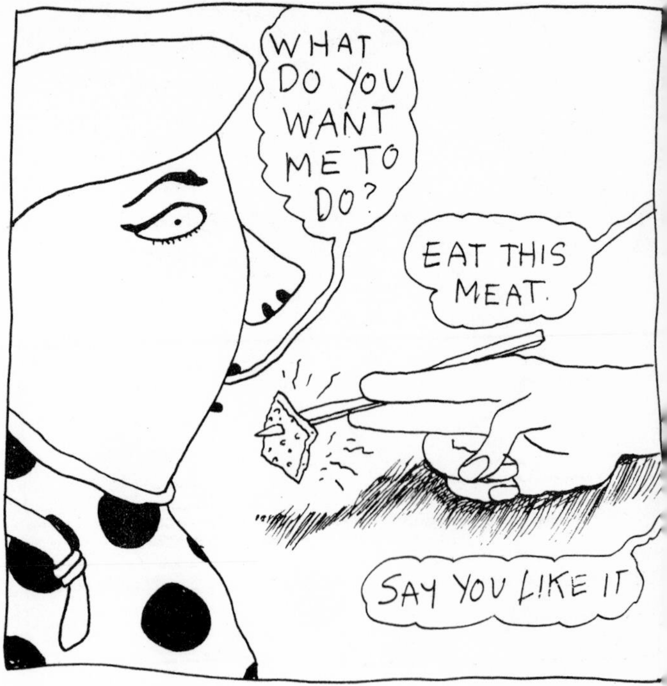
WHAT DO YOU WANT ME TO DO?
EAT THIS MEAT.
SAY YOU LIKE IT

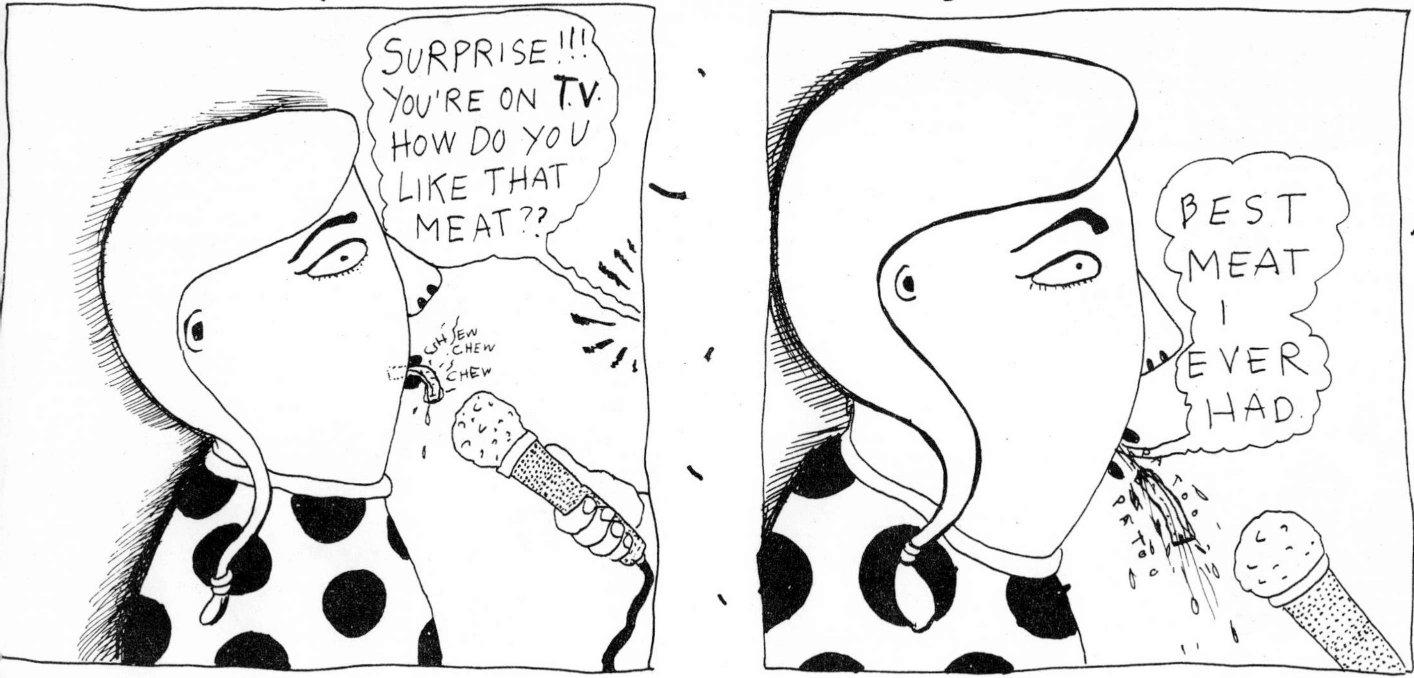
SURPRISE!!! YOU'RE ON T.V. HOW DO YOU LIKE THAT MEAT??
BEST MEAT I EVER HAD.

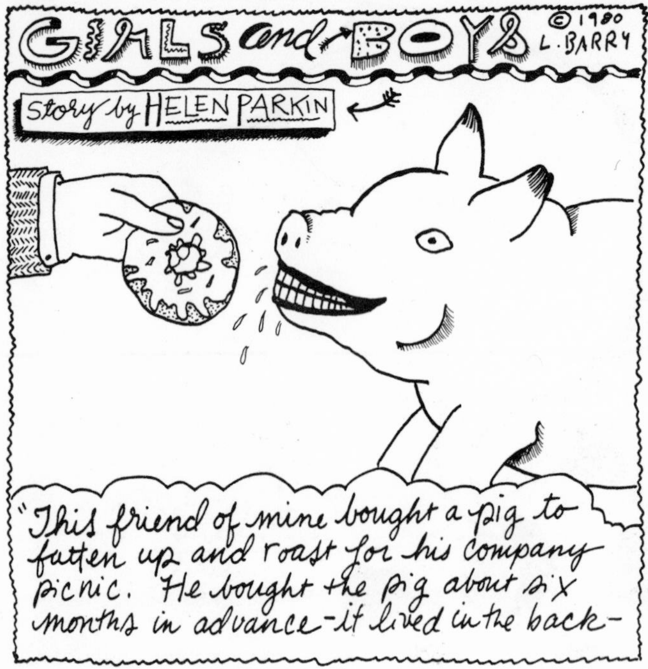
GIRLS and BOYS
©1980 L. BARRY
story by HELEN PARKIN
"This friend of mine bought a pig to fatten up and roast for his company picnic. He bought the pig about six months in advance - it lived in the back -

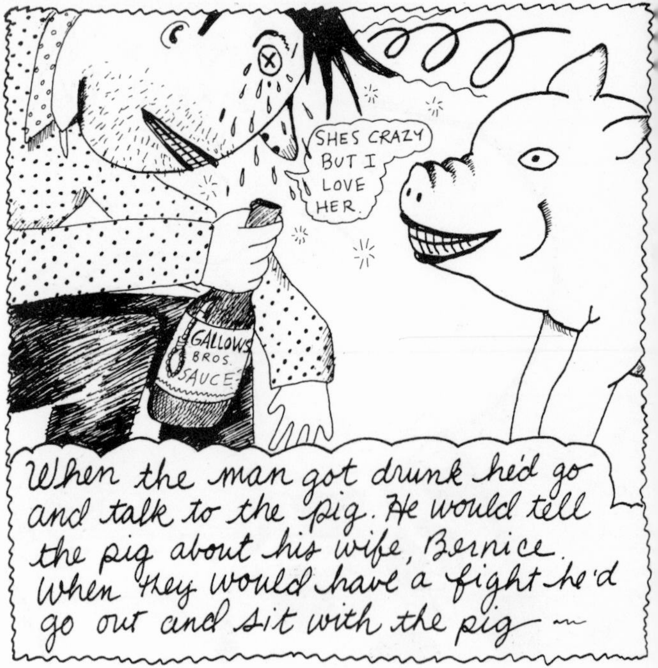
SHES CRAZY BUT I LOVE HER.
GALLOWS BROS. SAUCE
When the man got drunk he'd go and talk to the pig. He would tell the pig about his wife, Bernice. When they would have a fight he'd go out and sit with the pig --

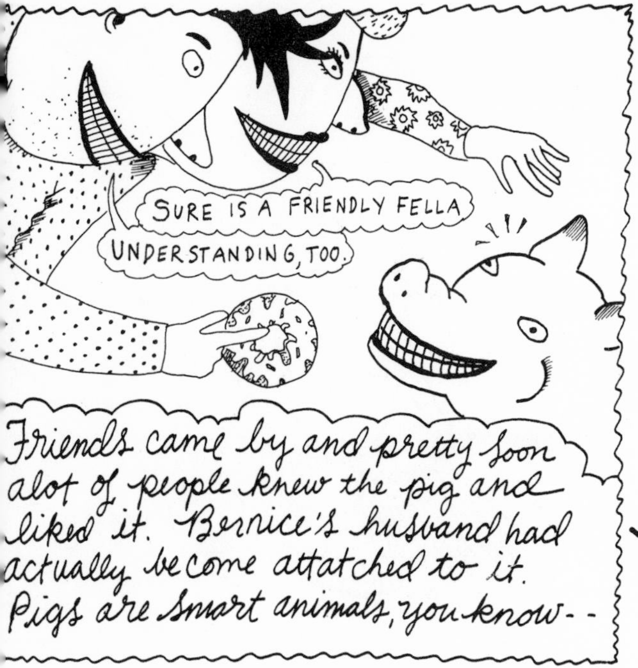
SURE IS A FRIENDLY FELLA
UNDERSTANDING, TOO.
Friends came by and pretty soon alot of people knew the pig and liked it. Bernice's husband had actually become attatched to it. Pigs are smart animals, you know- -

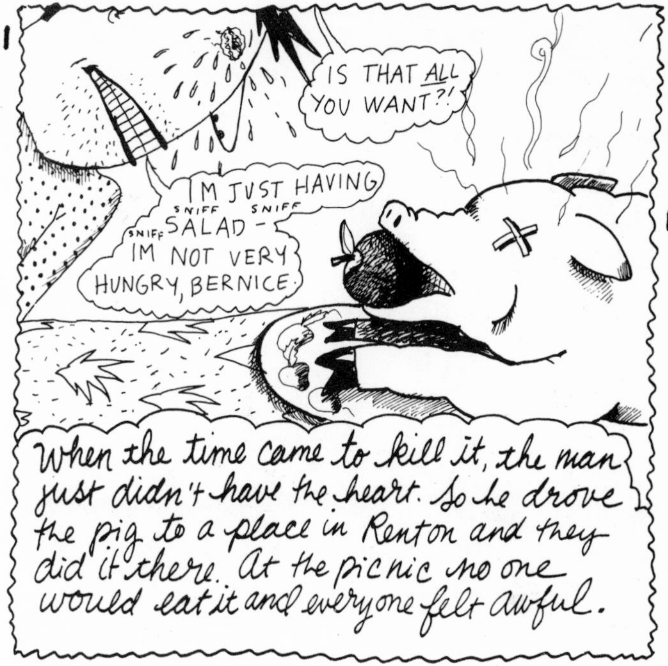
IS THAT ALL YOU WANT?!
I'M JUST HAVING SNIFF SNIFF SNIFF SALAD - I'M NOT VERY HUNGRY, BERNICE.
When the time came to kill it, the man just didn't have the heart. So he drove the pig to a place in Renton and they did it there. At the picnic no one would eat it and everyone felt awful.

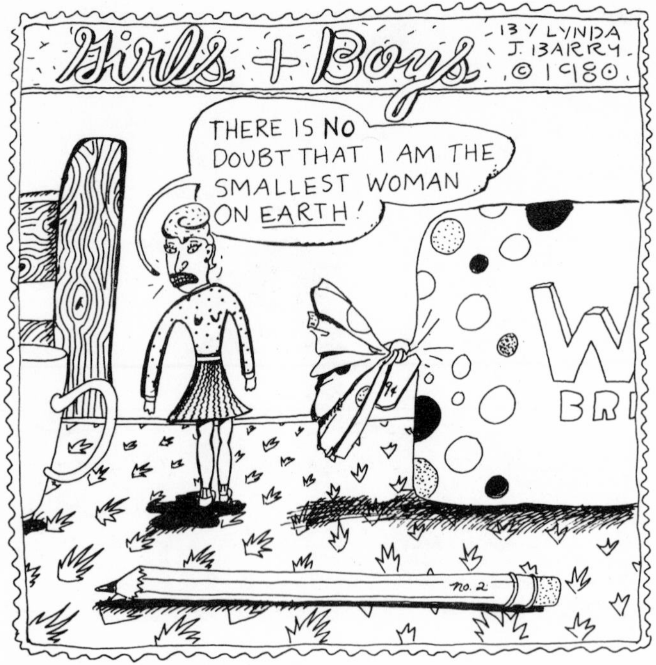
Girls + Boys
BY LYNDA J. BARRY ©1980
THERE IS NO DOUBT THAT I AM THE SMALLEST WOMAN ON EARTH!
no. 2

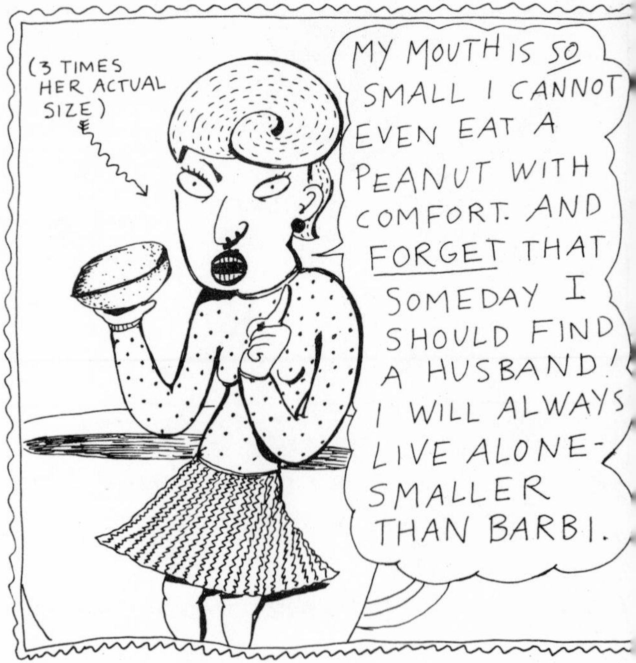
(3 TIMES HER ACTUAL SIZE)
MY MOUTH IS SO SMALL I CANNOT EVEN EAT A PEANUT WITH COMFORT. AND FORGET THAT SOMEDAY I SHOULD FIND A HUSBAND! I WILL ALWAYS LIVE ALONE- SMALLER THAN BARBI.

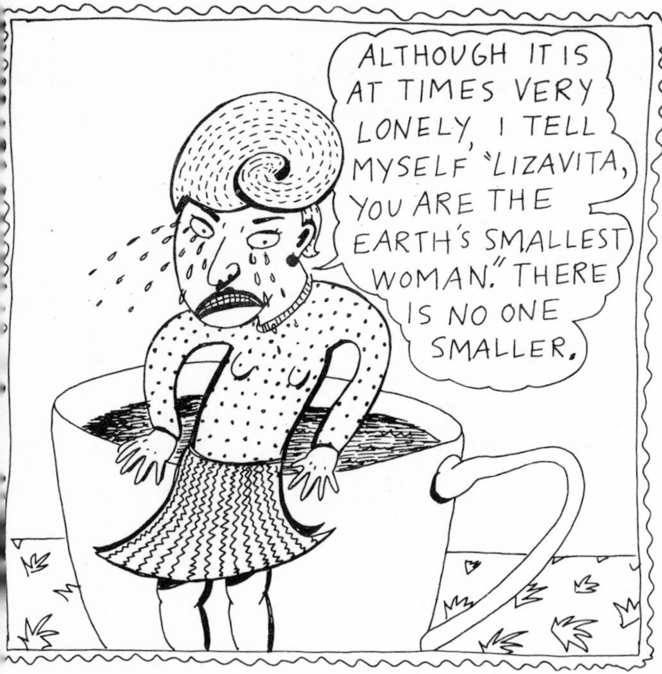
ALTHOUGH IT IS AT TIMES VERY LONELY, I TELL MYSELF "LIZAVITA, YOU ARE THE EARTH'S SMALLEST WOMAN." THERE IS NO ONE SMALLER.

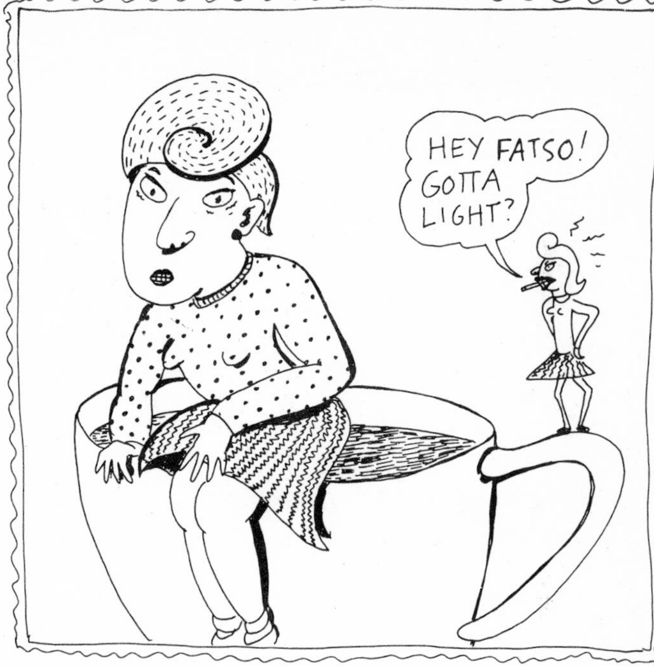
HEY FATSO! GOTTA LIGHT?

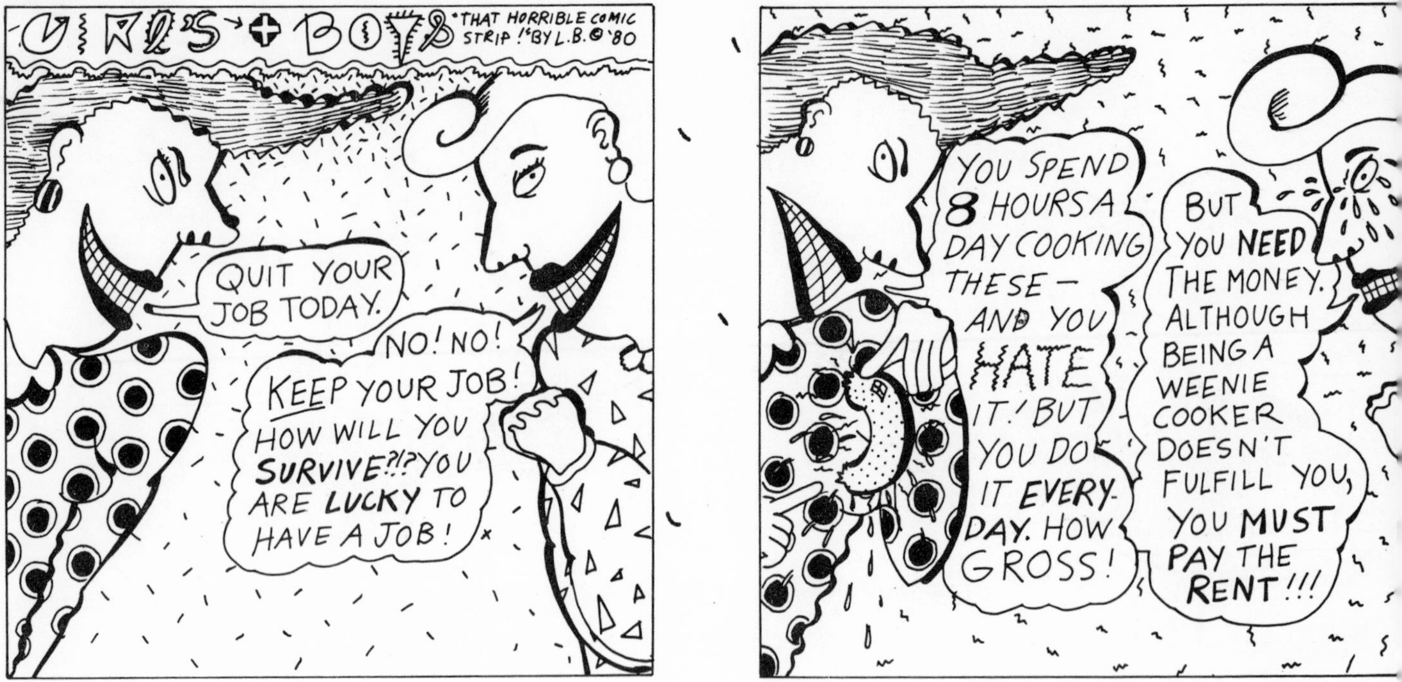
THAT HORRIBLE COMIC STRIP!" BY L.B. © '80
QUIT YOUR JOB TODAY.
NO! NO! KEEP YOUR JOB! HOW WILL YOU SURVIVE?!? YOU ARE LUCKY TO HAVE A JOB!
YOU SPEND 8 HOURS A DAY COOKING THESE — AND YOU HATE IT! BUT YOU DO IT EVERY-DAY. HOW GROSS!
BUT YOU NEED THE MONEY. ALTHOUGH BEING A WEENIE COOKER DOESN'T FULFILL YOU, YOU MUST PAY THE RENT!!!

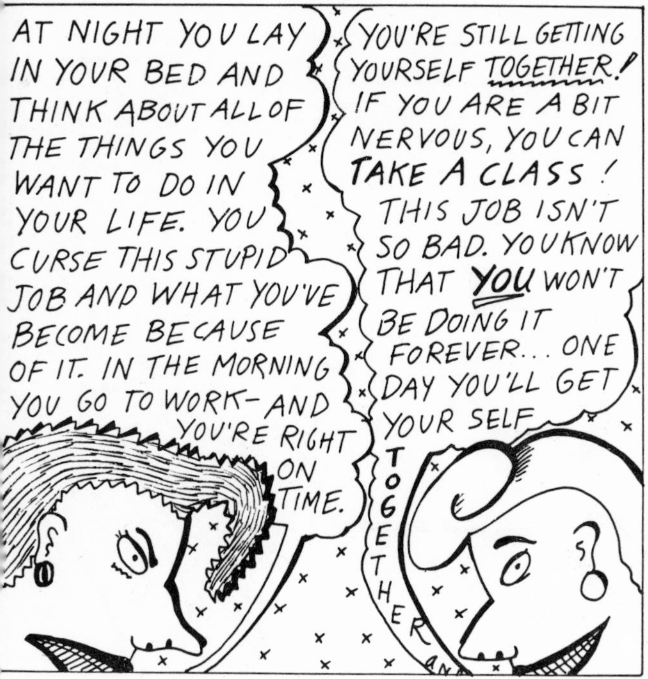
AT NIGHT YOU LAY IN YOUR BED AND THINK ABOUT ALL OF THE THINGS YOU WANT TO DO IN YOUR LIFE. YOU CURSE THIS STUPID JOB AND WHAT YOU'VE BECOME BECAUSE OF IT. IN THE MORNING YOU GO TO WORK– AND YOU'RE RIGHT ON TIME.
YOU'RE STILL GETTING YOURSELF TOGETHER! IF YOU ARE A BIT NERVOUS, YOU CAN TAKE A CLASS! THIS JOB ISN'T SO BAD. YOU KNOW THAT **YOU** WON'T BE DOING IT FOREVER... ONE DAY YOU'LL GET YOUR SELF TOGETHER

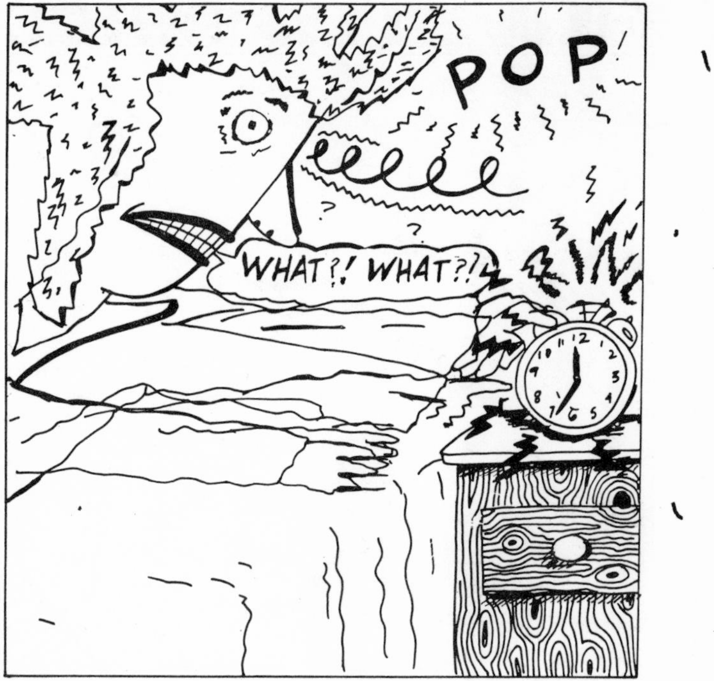
POP!
WHAT?! WHAT?!

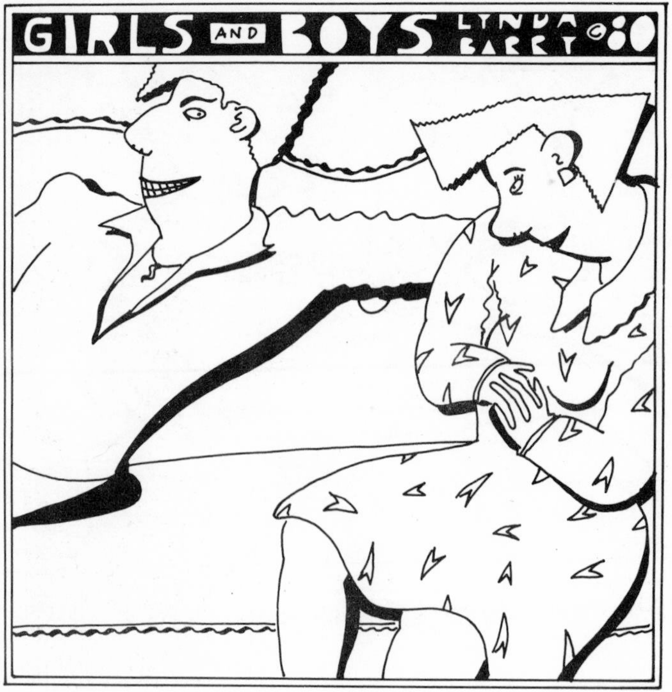
GIRLS AND BOYS
LYNDA BARRY ©80

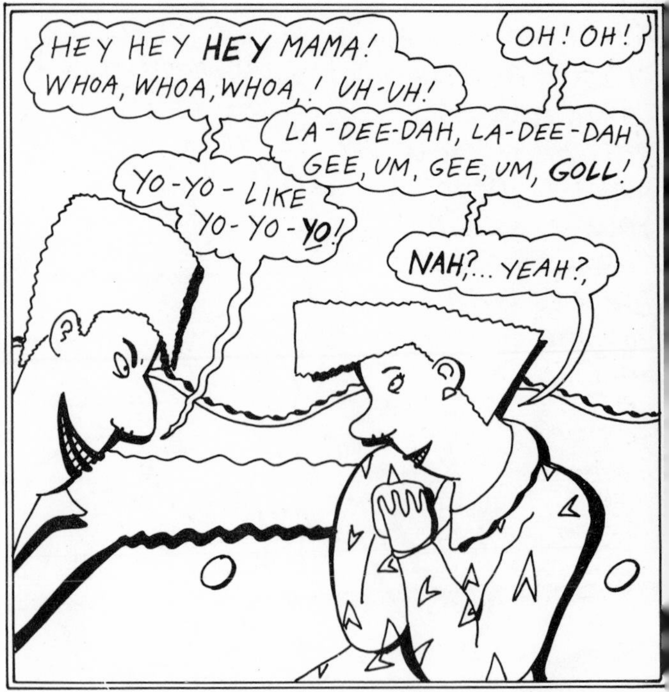
HEY HEY HEY MAMA! WHOA, WHOA, WHOA! UH-UH!
OH! OH!
LA-DEE-DAH, LA-DEE-DAH GEE, UM, GEE, UM, GOLL!
YO-YO-LIKE YO-YO-YO!
NAH?... YEAH?

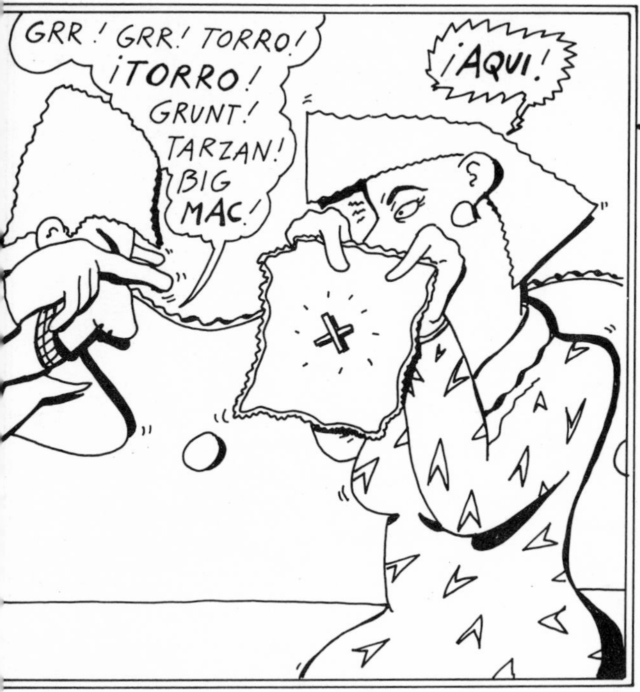
GRR! GRR! TORRO! ¡TORRO! GRUNT! TARZAN! BIG MAC!
¡AQUI!

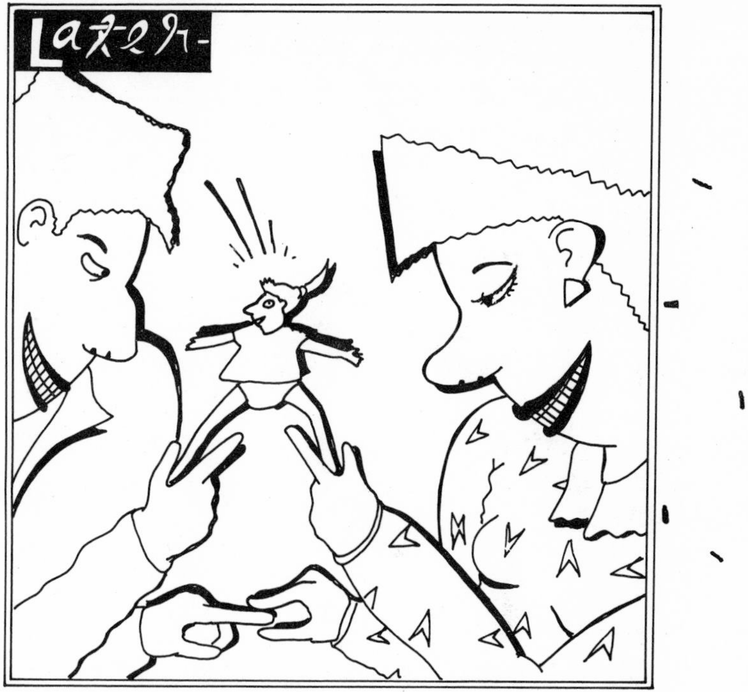

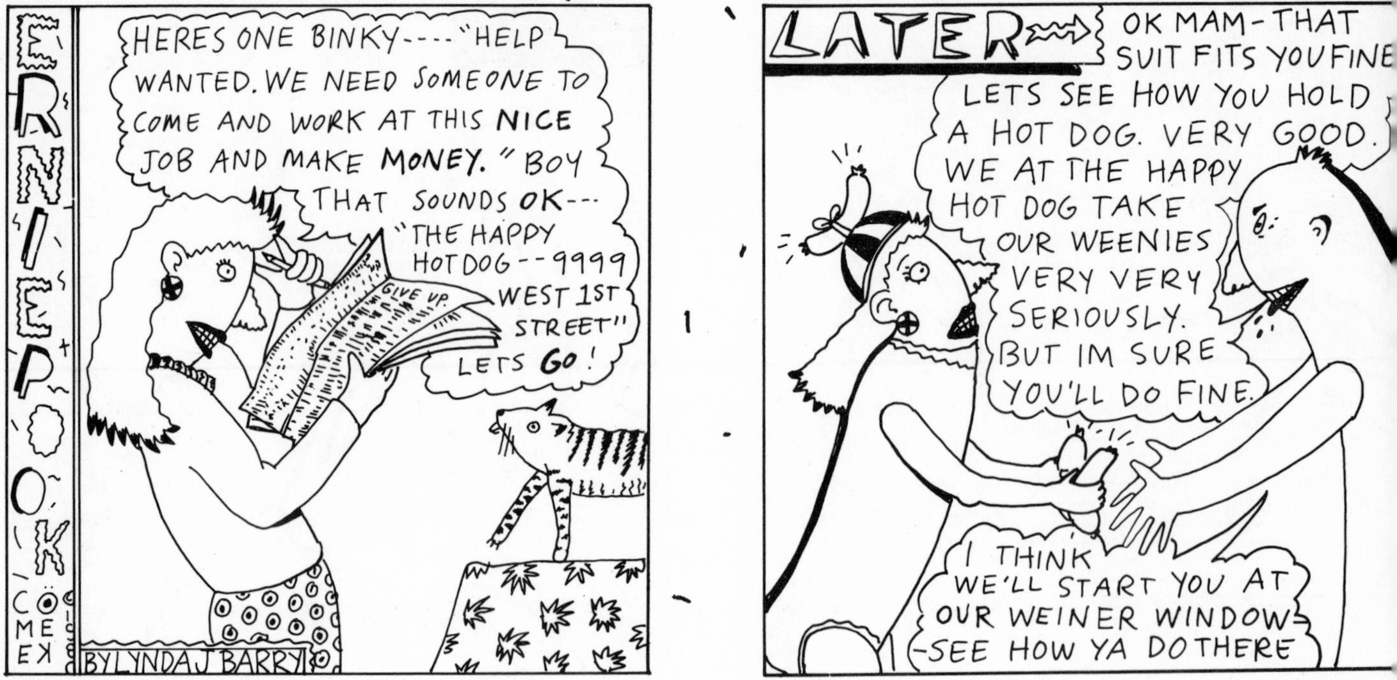
ERNIE POOK
COMEEK
BY LYNDA J BARRY
HERES ONE BINKY---- "HELP WANTED. WE NEED SOMEONE TO COME AND WORK AT THIS NICE JOB AND MAKE MONEY." BOY THAT SOUNDS OK--- "THE HAPPY HOTDOG--9999 WEST 1ST STREET" LETS GO!
GIVE UP.
LATER
OK MAM-THAT SUIT FITS YOU FINE
LETS SEE HOW YOU HOLD A HOT DOG. VERY GOOD. WE AT THE HAPPY HOT DOG TAKE OUR WEENIES VERY VERY SERIOUSLY. BUT IM SURE YOU'LL DO FINE.
I THINK WE'LL START YOU AT OUR WEINER WINDOW-SEE HOW YA DO THERE

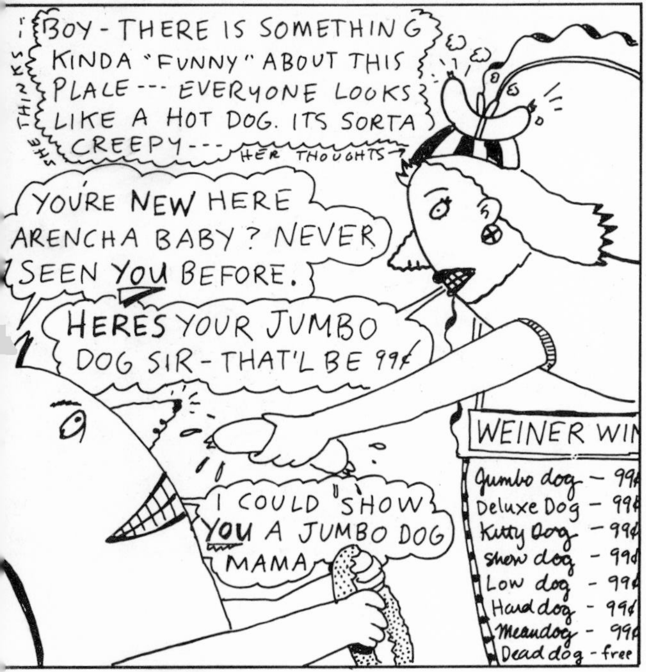
SHE THINKS
BOY - THERE IS SOMETHING KINDA "FUNNY" ABOUT THIS PLACE --- EVERYONE LOOKS LIKE A HOT DOG. ITS SORTA CREEPY---
HER THOUGHTS
YOU'RE NEW HERE ARENCHA BABY? NEVER SEEN YOU BEFORE.
HERES YOUR JUMBO DOG SIR - THAT'L BE 99¢
I COULD SHOW YOU A JUMBO DOG MAMA
WEINER WI
Jumbo dog - 99¢
Deluxe Dog - 99¢
Kitty Dog - 99¢
show dog - 99¢
Low dog - 99¢
Hard dog - 99¢
Meandog - 99¢
Dead dog - free

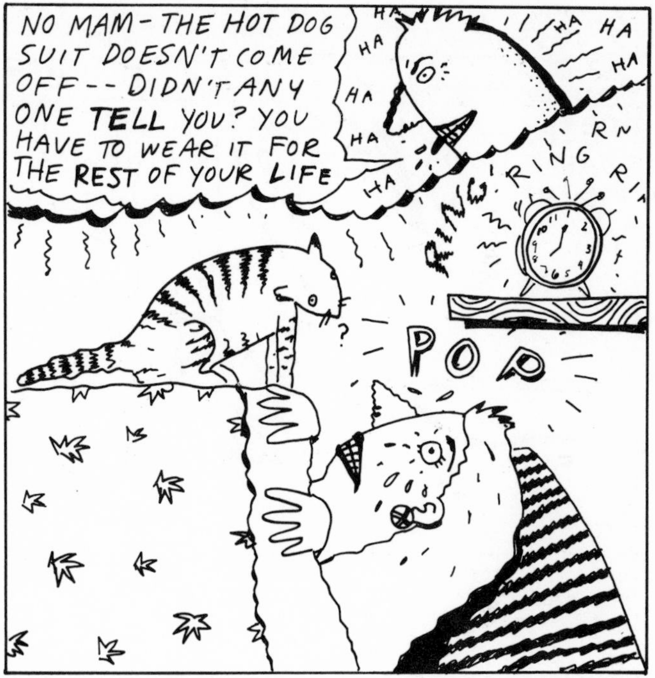
NO MAM - THE HOT DOG SUIT DOESN'T COME OFF -- DIDN'T ANY ONE TELL YOU? YOU HAVE TO WEAR IT FOR THE REST OF YOUR LIFE
HA HA HA HA HA HA HA HA
RING! RING RING
POP

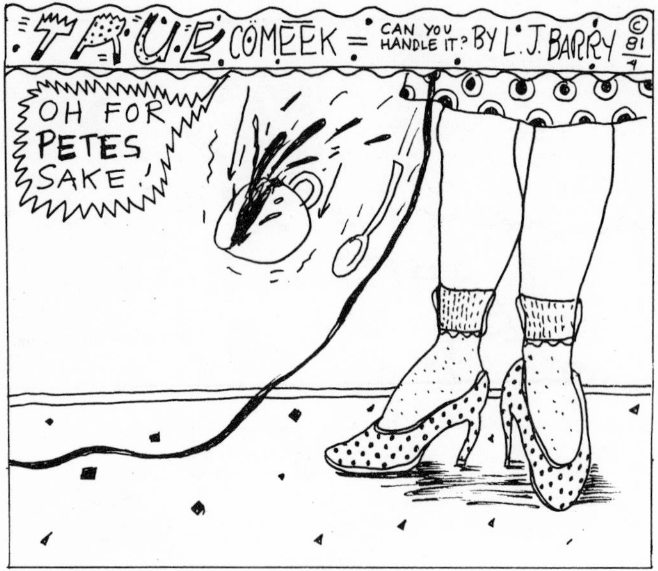
TRUE COMEEK = CAN YOU HANDLE IT? BY L. J. BARRY © 81
OH FOR PETES SAKE!

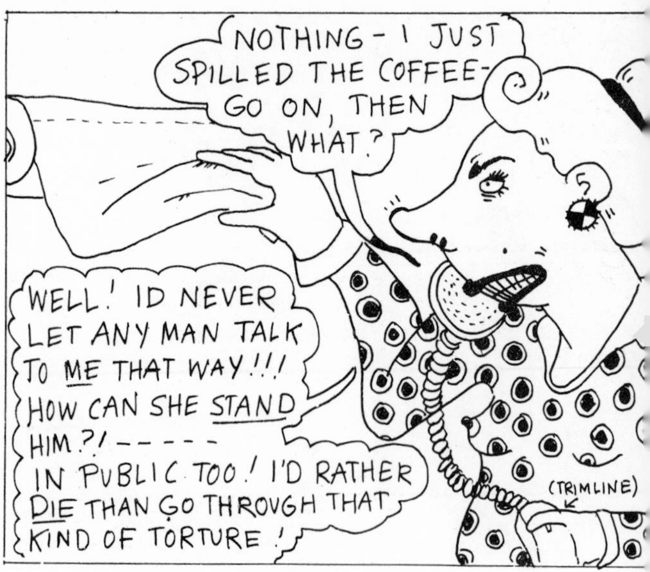
NOTHING - I JUST SPILLED THE COFFEE- GO ON, THEN WHAT?
WELL! ID NEVER LET ANY MAN TALK TO ME THAT WAY!!! HOW CAN SHE STAND HIM?! -----
IN PUBLIC TOO! I'D RATHER DIE THAN GO THROUGH THAT KIND OF TORTURE!
(TRIMLINE)

WHAT??
BOY, I'LL SAY. NO KIDDIN. NOT THIS LADY! NO SIR. SINGLE LIFE IS JUST FINE WITH ME. WHO WANTS THAT KIND OF GRIEF FOR CRISSAKES?? SO YOU GOTTA DATE TANITE? WANNA PLAY CARDS? —OH. WITH THAT SCHMOE MARTY? I DON'T KNOW HOW YOU CAN STAND THAT GUY. O.K. ITS YOUR FUNERAL. O.K. I'LL SEE YA GIGI, BYE.

CLICK

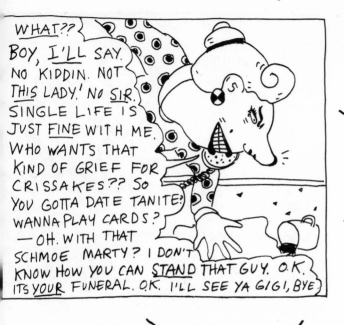

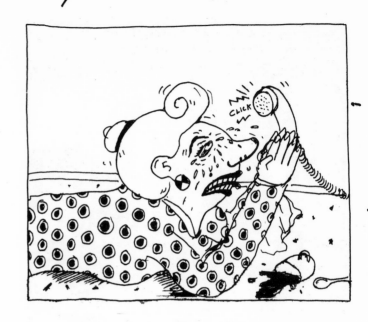

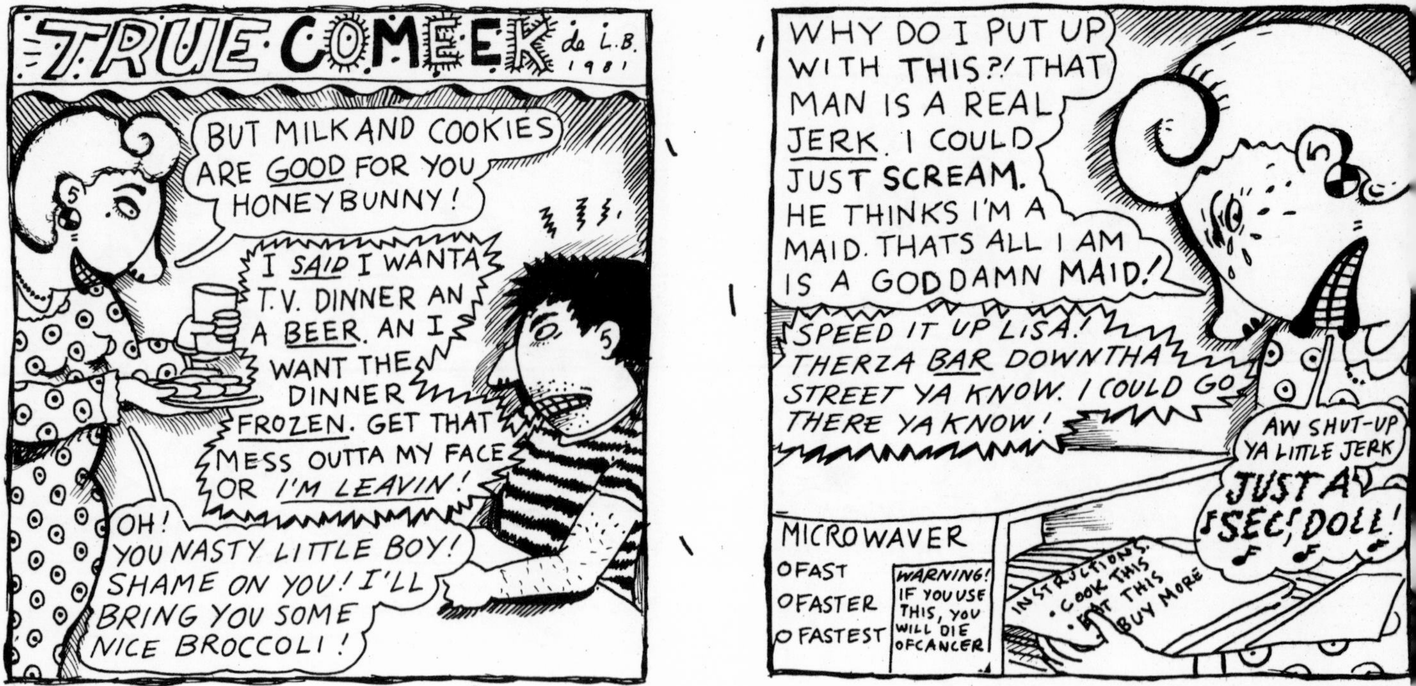
TRUE COMEEK
de L.B. 1981
BUT MILK AND COOKIES ARE GOOD FOR YOU HONEYBUNNY!
I SAID I WANTA T.V. DINNER AN A BEER. AN I WANT THE DINNER FROZEN. GET THAT MESS OUTTA MY FACE OR I'M LEAVIN!
OH! YOU NASTY LITTLE BOY! SHAME ON YOU! I'LL BRING YOU SOME NICE BROCCOLI!
WHY DO I PUT UP WITH THIS?! THAT MAN IS A REAL JERK. I COULD JUST SCREAM. HE THINKS I'M A MAID. THATS ALL I AM IS A GODDAMN MAID!
SPEED IT UP LISA! THERZA BAR DOWNTHA STREET YA KNOW. I COULD GO THERE YA KNOW!
AW SHUT-UP YA LITTLE JERK
JUST A SEC, DOLL!
MICROWAVER
FAST
FASTER
FASTEST
WARNING! IF YOU USE THIS, YOU WILL DIE OF CANCER
INSTRUCTIONS. • COOK THIS • EAT THIS BUY MORE

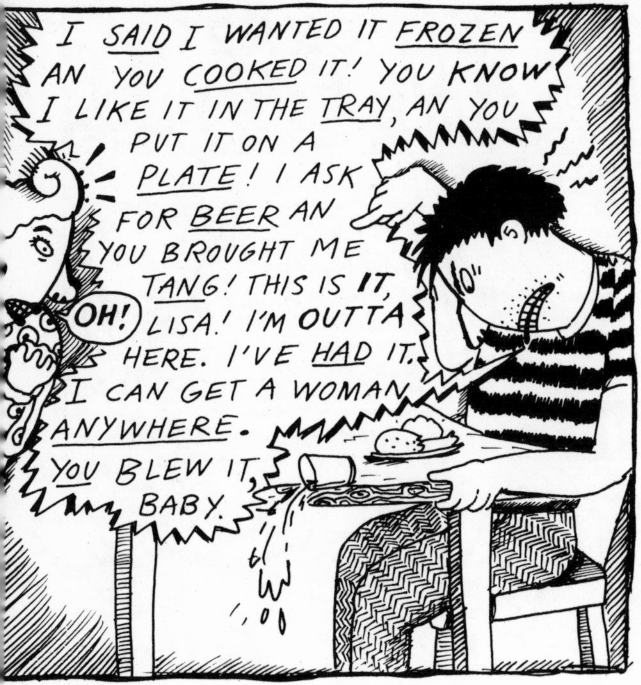
I SAID I WANTED IT FROZEN AN YOU COOKED IT! YOU KNOW I LIKE IT IN THE TRAY, AN YOU PUT IT ON A PLATE! I ASK FOR BEER AN YOU BROUGHT ME TANG! THIS IS IT, LISA! I'M OUTTA HERE. I'VE HAD IT. I CAN GET A WOMAN ANYWHERE. YOU BLEW IT, BABY.
OH!

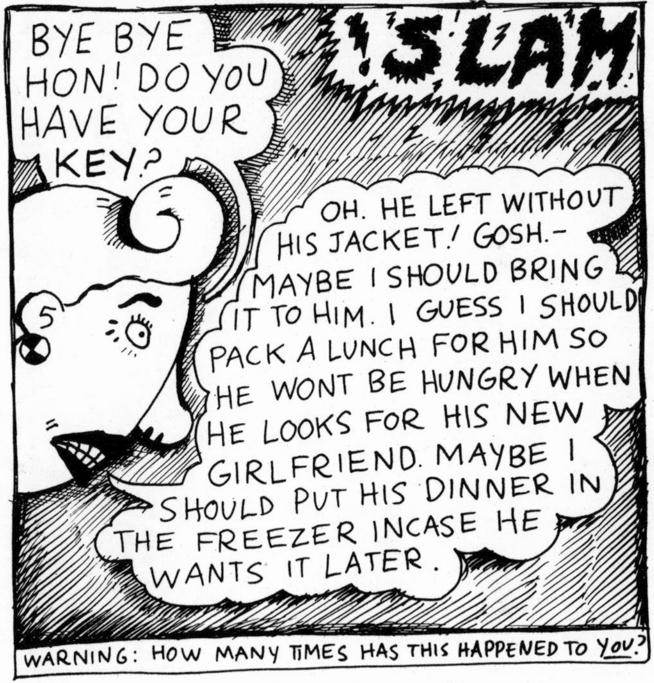
BYE BYE HON! DO YOU HAVE YOUR KEY?
SLAM
OH. HE LEFT WITHOUT HIS JACKET! GOSH.- MAYBE I SHOULD BRING IT TO HIM. I GUESS I SHOULD PACK A LUNCH FOR HIM SO HE WONT BE HUNGRY WHEN HE LOOKS FOR HIS NEW GIRLFRIEND. MAYBE I SHOULD PUT HIS DINNER IN THE FREEZER INCASE HE WANTS IT LATER.

WARNING: HOW MANY TIMES HAS THIS HAPPENED TO YOU?

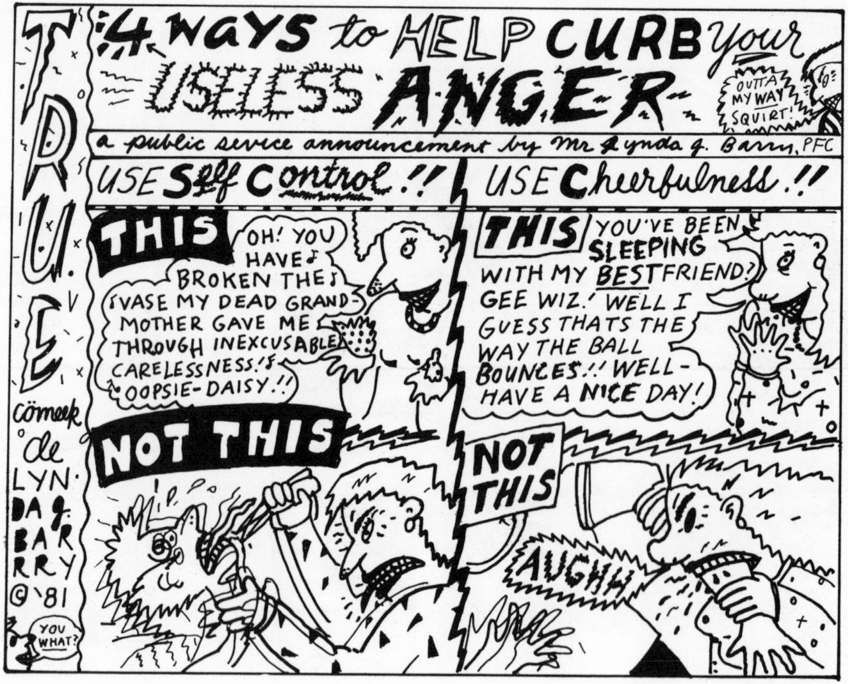
TRUE
4 WAYS to HELP CURB your USELESS ANGER
OUTTA MY WAY SQUIRT!
a public sevice announcement by Mr Lynda J. Barry, PFC
USE Self Control!!
THIS
OH! YOU HAVE BROKEN THE VASE MY DEAD GRANDMOTHER GAVE ME THROUGH INEXCUSABLE CARELESSNESS! OOPSIE-DAISY!!
NOT THIS
USE Cheerfulness!!
THIS
YOU'VE BEEN SLEEPING WITH MY BESTFRIEND? GEE WIZ! WELL I GUESS THATS THE WAY THE BALL BOUNCES!! WELL-HAVE A NICE DAY!
NOT THIS
AUGHH
cömeek de LYNDA J. BARRY © '81
YOU WHAT?

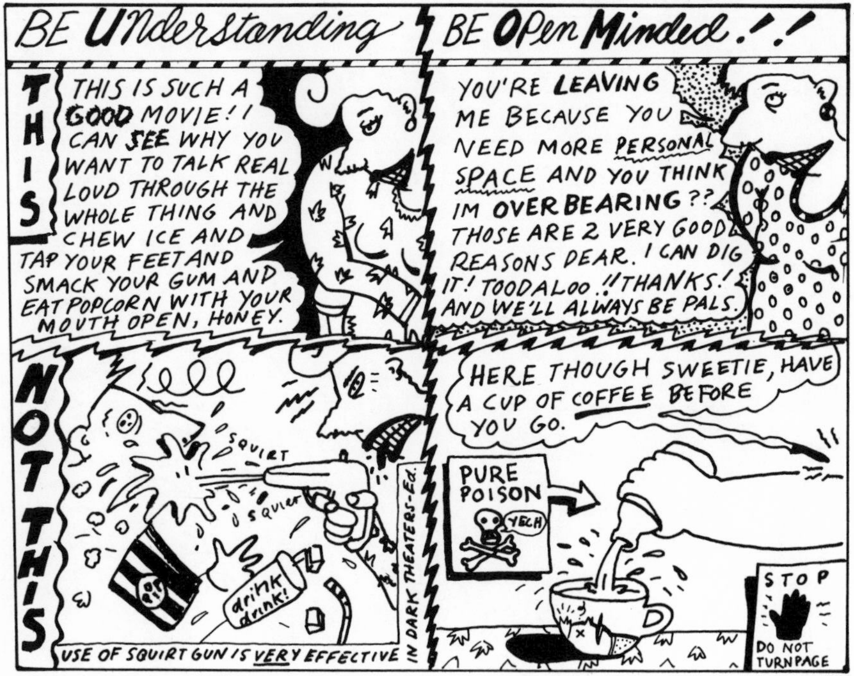
BE UNderstanding
BE OPen Minded.!.!
THIS
THIS IS SUCH A GOOD MOVIE!! CAN SEE WHY YOU WANT TO TALK REAL LOUD THROUGH THE WHOLE THING AND CHEW ICE AND TAP YOUR FEET AND SMACK YOUR GUM AND EAT POPCORN WITH YOUR MOUTH OPEN, HONEY.
YOU'RE LEAVING ME BECAUSE YOU NEED MORE PERSONAL SPACE AND YOU THINK IM OVERBEARING?? THOSE ARE 2 VERY GOOD REASONS DEAR. I CAN DIG IT! TOODALOO!! THANKS! AND WE'LL ALWAYS BE PALS.
NOT THIS
SQUIRT
SQUIRT
drink drink!
USE OF SQUIRT GUN IS VERY EFFECTIVE
IN DARK THEATERS-Ed.
HERE THOUGH SWEETIE, HAVE A CUP OF COFFEE BEFORE YOU GO.
PURE POISON
YECH
STOP
DO NOT TURNPAGE

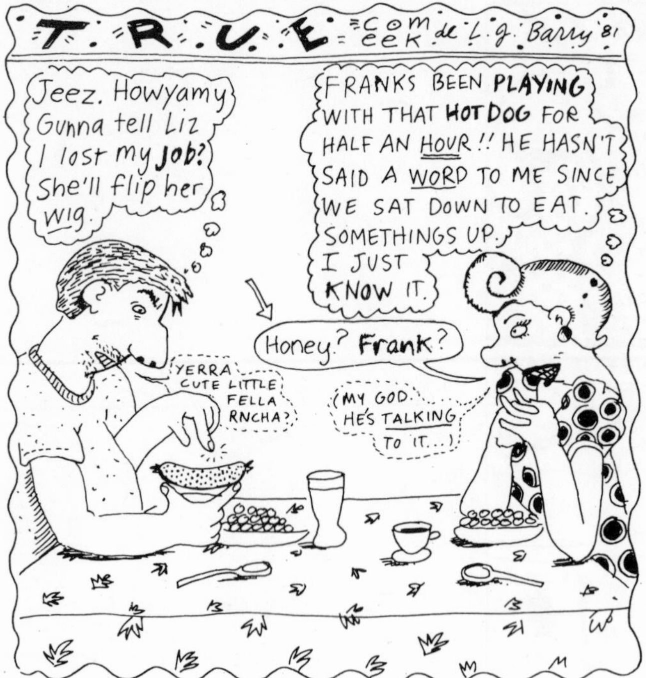
T.R.U.E com eek de L.J. Barry '81
Jeez. Howyamy Gunna tell Liz I lost my JOB? She'll flip her wig.
FRANKS BEEN PLAYING WITH THAT HOT DOG FOR HALF AN HOUR!! HE HASN'T SAID A WORD TO ME SINCE WE SAT DOWN TO EAT. SOMETHINGS UP. I JUST KNOW IT.
Honey? Frank?
YERRA CUTE LITTLE FELLA RNCHA?
(MY GOD. HE'S TALKING TO IT...)

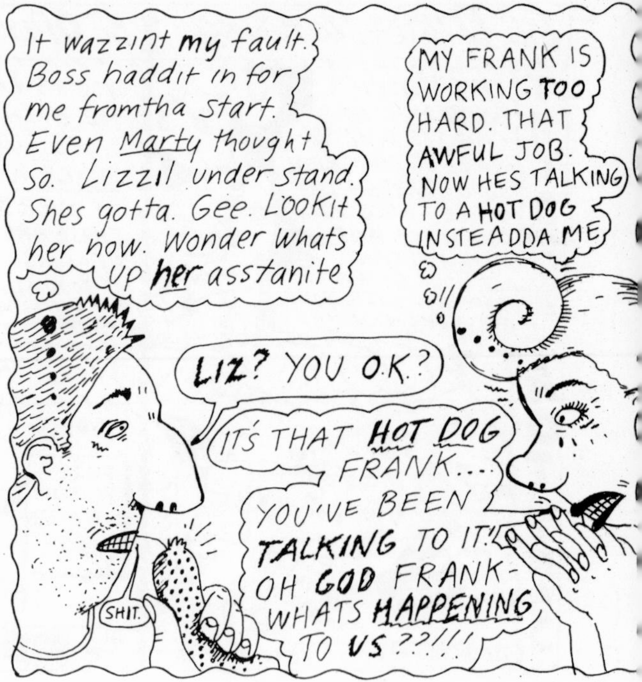
It wazzint my fault. Boss haddit in for me fromtha start. Even Marty thought so. Lizzil under stand. Shes gotta. Gee. Lookit her now. Wonder whats up her asstanite
MY FRANK IS WORKING TOO HARD. THAT AWFUL JOB. NOW HES TALKING TO A HOT DOG INSTEADDA ME
LIZ? YOU O.K?
IT'S THAT HOT DOG FRANK... YOU'VE BEEN TALKING TO IT! OH GOD FRANK- WHATS HAPPENING TO US??!!!
SHIT.

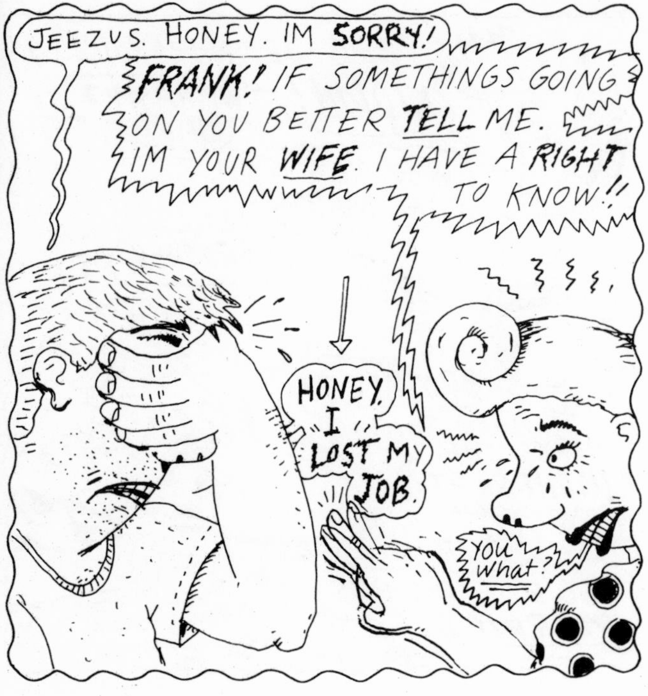
JEEZUS. HONEY. IM SORRY!
FRANK! IF SOMETHINGS GOING ON YOU BETTER TELL ME. IM YOUR WIFE. I HAVE A RIGHT TO KNOW!!
HONEY. I LOST MY JOB.
YOU what?

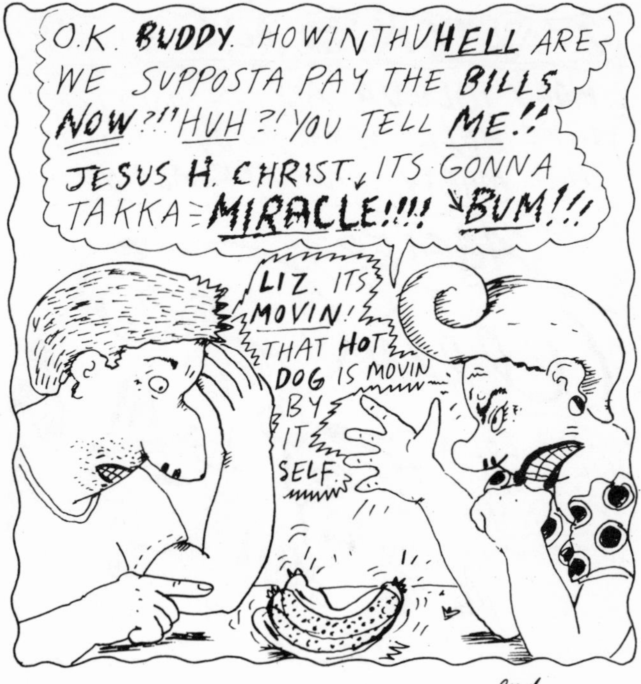
O.K. BUDDY. HOWINTHUHELL ARE WE SUPPOSTA PAY THE BILLS NOW?!! HUH?! YOU TELL ME!!
JESUS H. CHRIST. ITS GONNA TAKKA MIRACLE!!!! BUM!!!
LIZ. ITS MOVIN! THAT HOT DOG IS MOVIN BY IT SELF.

end

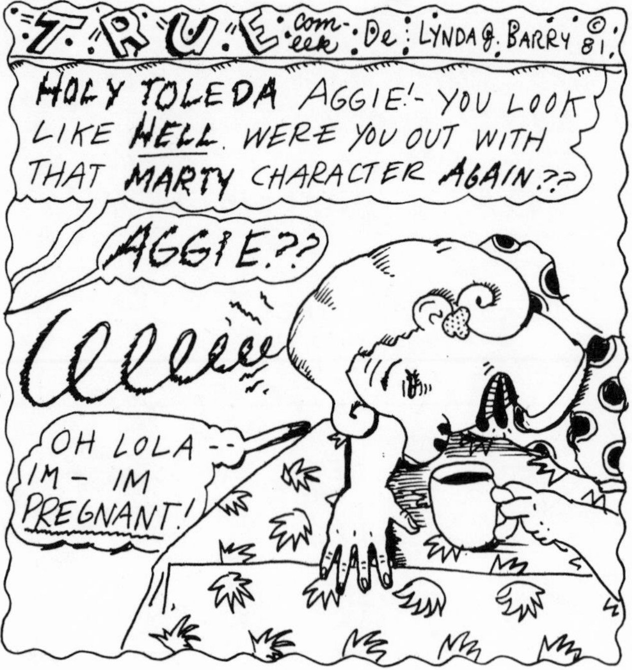
TRUE com-eek De Lynda J. Barry © 81.
HOLY TOLEDA AGGIE!- YOU LOOK LIKE HELL. WERE YOU OUT WITH THAT MARTY CHARACTER AGAIN??
AGGIE??
Wwwww
OH LOLA-- IM- IM PREGNANT!

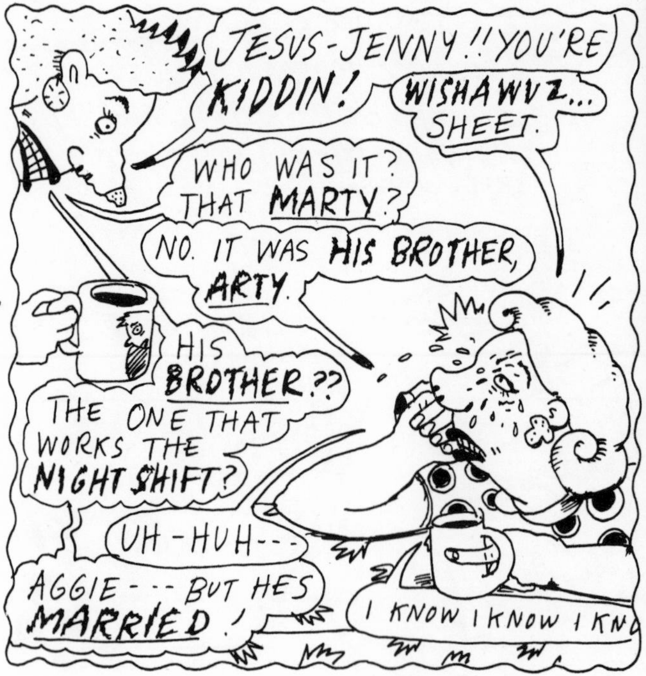
JESUS-JENNY!! YOU'RE KIDDIN!
WISHAWUZ... SHEET.
WHO WAS IT? THAT MARTY?
NO. IT WAS HIS BROTHER, ARTY.
HIS BROTHER??
THE ONE THAT WORKS THE NIGHT SHIFT?
UH-HUH---
AGGIE--- BUT HES MARRIED!
I KNOW I KNOW I KN

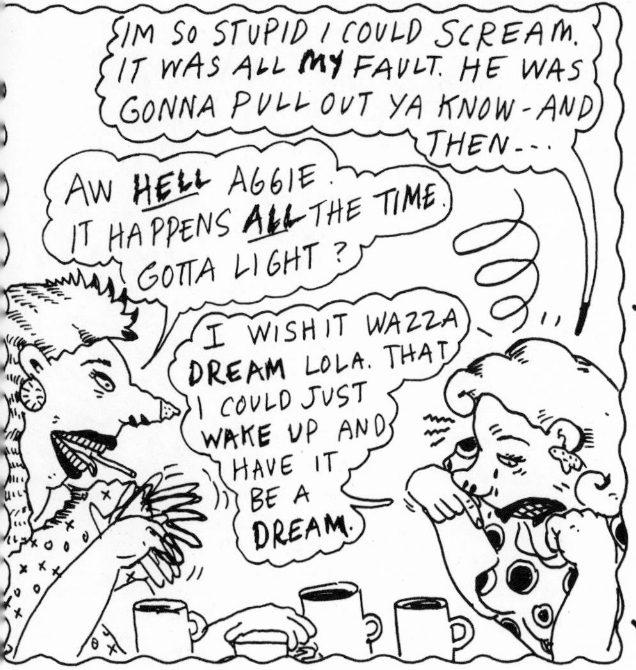
IM SO STUPID I COULD SCREAM. IT WAS ALL MY FAULT. HE WAS GONNA PULL OUT YA KNOW - AND THEN...
AW HELL AGGIE. IT HAPPENS ALL THE TIME. GOTTA LIGHT?
I WISH IT WAZZA DREAM LOLA. THAT I COULD JUST WAKE UP AND HAVE IT BE A DREAM.

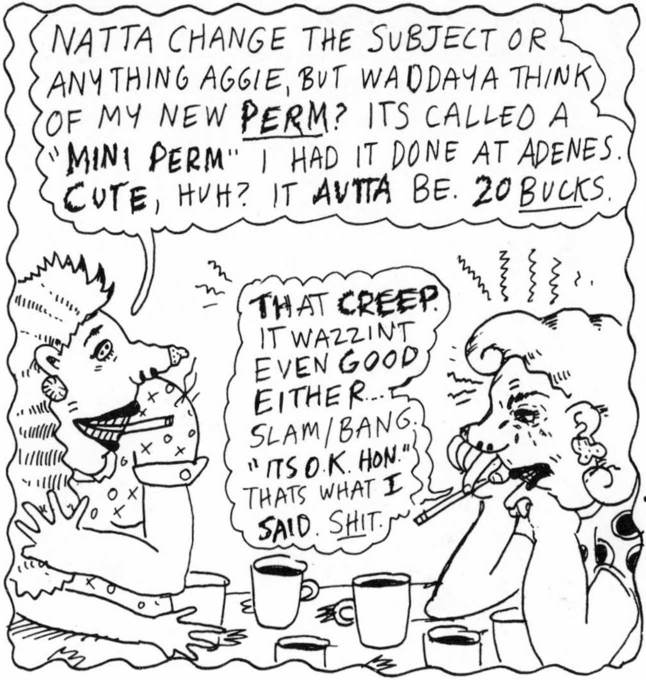
NATTA CHANGE THE SUBJECT OR ANYTHING AGGIE, BUT WADDAYA THINK OF MY NEW PERM? ITS CALLED A "MINI PERM" I HAD IT DONE AT ADENES. CUTE, HUH? IT AUTTA BE. 20 BUCKS.
THAT CREEP. IT WAZZINT EVEN GOOD EITHER... SLAM/BANG. "ITS O.K. HON." THATS WHAT I SAID. SHIT.

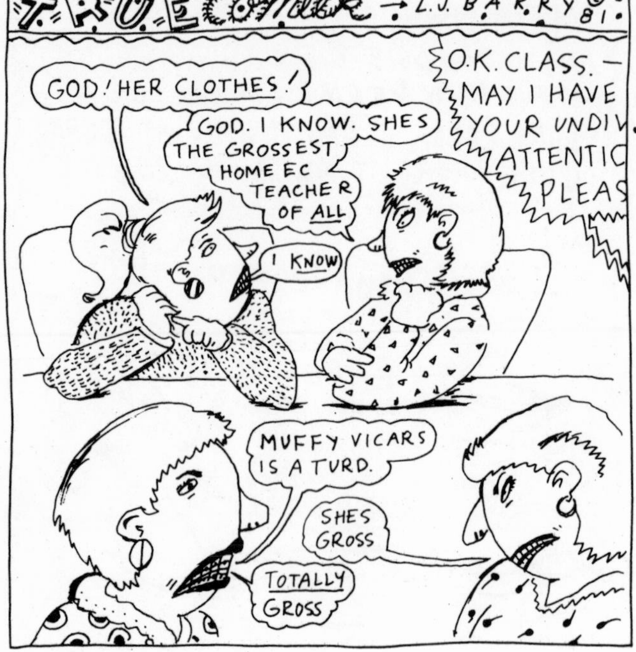
T.R.U.E.
L.J. BARRY ©81
O.K. CLASS. — MAY I HAVE YOUR UNDIV ATTENTIC PLEAS
GOD! HER CLOTHES!
GOD. I KNOW. SHES THE GROSSEST HOME EC TEACHER OF ALL
I KNOW
MUFFY VICARS IS A TURD.
SHES GROSS
TOTALLY GROSS

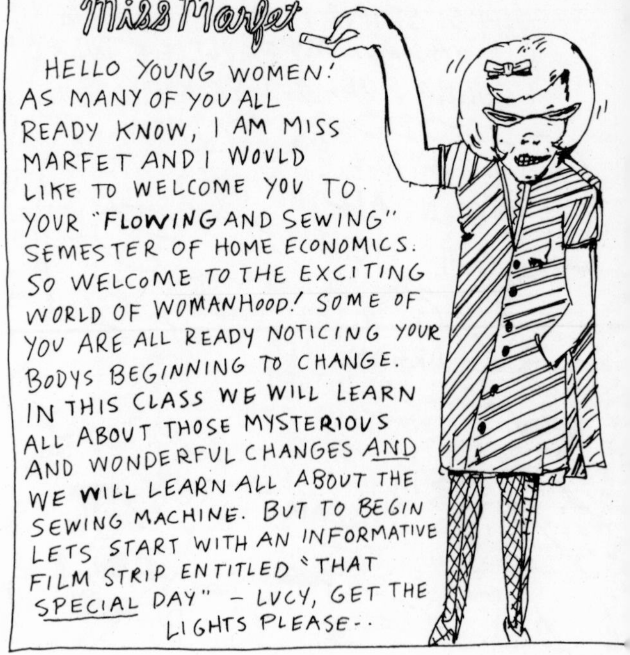
Miss Marfet
HELLO YOUNG WOMEN! AS MANY OF YOU ALL READY KNOW, I AM MISS MARFET AND I WOULD LIKE TO WELCOME YOU TO YOUR "FLOWING AND SEWING" SEMESTER OF HOME ECONOMICS. SO WELCOME TO THE EXCITING WORLD OF WOMANHOOD! SOME OF YOU ARE ALL READY NOTICING YOUR BODYS BEGINNING TO CHANGE. IN THIS CLASS WE WILL LEARN ALL ABOUT THOSE MYSTERIOUS AND WONDERFUL CHANGES AND WE WILL LEARN ALL ABOUT THE SEWING MACHINE. BUT TO BEGIN LETS START WITH AN INFORMATIVE FILM STRIP ENTITLED "THAT SPECIAL DAY" — LUCY, GET THE LIGHTS PLEASE..

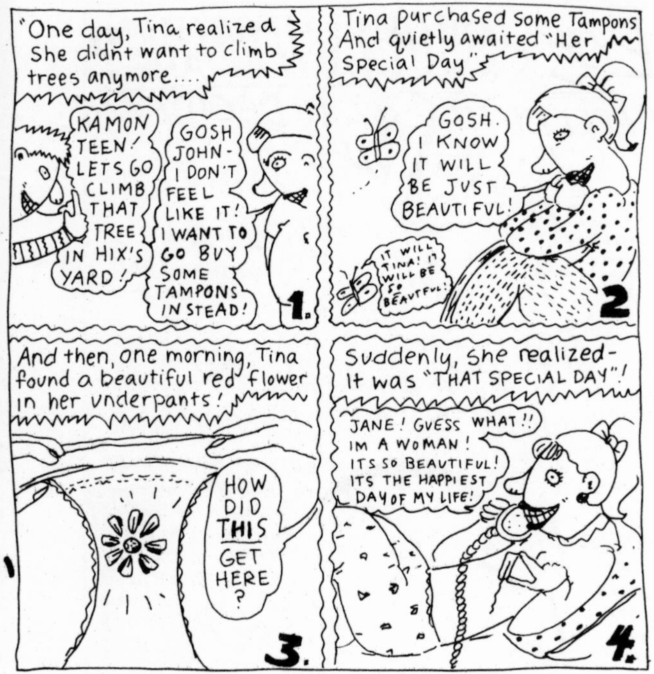
"One day, Tina realized She didn't want to climb trees anymore....
KAMON TEEN! LETS GO CLIMB THAT TREE IN HIX'S YARD!
GOSH JOHN- I DON'T FEEL LIKE IT! I WANT TO GO BUY SOME TAMPONS INSTEAD!
1.
Tina purchased some Tampons And quietly awaited "Her Special Day"
GOSH. I KNOW IT WILL BE JUST BEAUTIFUL!
IT WILL TINA! IT WILL BE SO BEAUTFUL!
2
And then, one morning, Tina found a beautiful red flower in her underpants!
HOW DID THIS GET HERE ?
3.
Suddenly, she realized- It was "THAT SPECIAL DAY"!
JANE! GUESS WHAT!! IM A WOMAN! ITS SO BEAUTIFUL! ITS THE HAPPIEST DAY OF MY LIFE!
4.

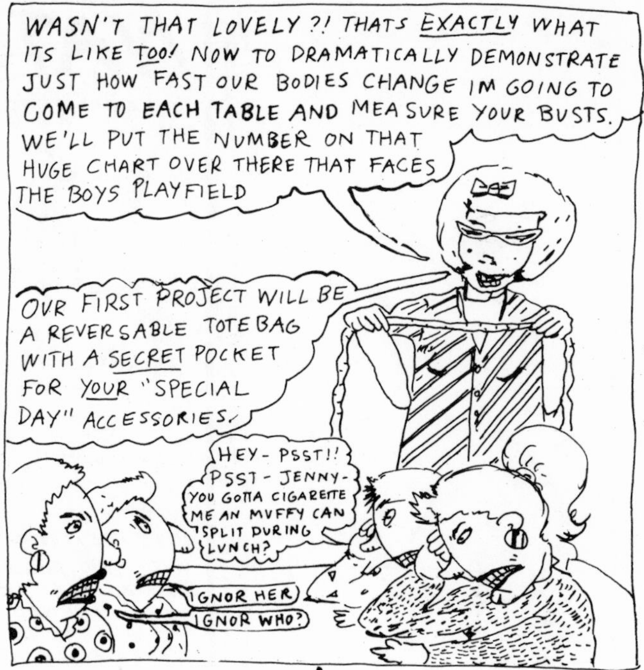
WASN'T THAT LOVELY?! THATS EXACTLY WHAT ITS LIKE TOO! NOW TO DRAMATICALLY DEMONSTRATE JUST HOW FAST OUR BODIES CHANGE IM GOING TO COME TO EACH TABLE AND MEASURE YOUR BUSTS. WE'LL PUT THE NUMBER ON THAT HUGE CHART OVER THERE THAT FACES THE BOYS PLAYFIELD
OUR FIRST PROJECT WILL BE A REVERSABLE TOTE BAG WITH A SECRET POCKET FOR YOUR "SPECIAL DAY" ACCESSORIES.
HEY- PSST!! PSST - JENNY- YOU GOTTA CIGARETTE ME AN MUFFY CAN SPLIT DURING LUNCH?
IGNOR HER
IGNOR WHO?

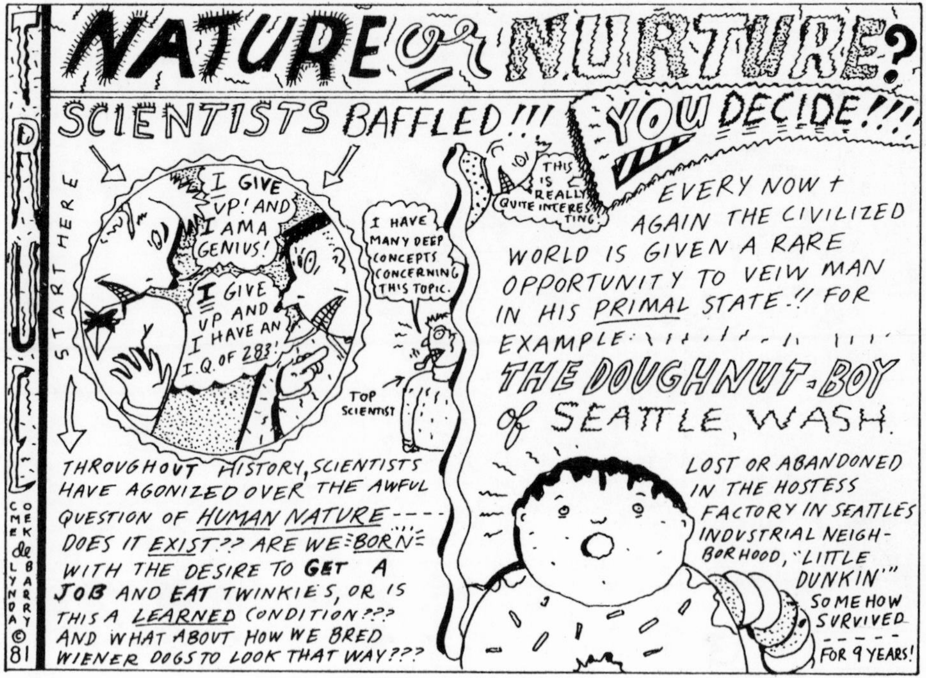
NATURE or NURTURE?
SCIENTISTS BAFFLED!!!
YOU DECIDE!!!
START HERE
I GIVE UP! AND I AM A GENIUS!
I GIVE UP AND I HAVE AN I.Q. OF 283!
I HAVE MANY DEEP CONCEPTS CONCERNING THIS TOPIC.
TOP SCIENTIST
THIS IS REALLY QUITE INTERESTING!
EVERY NOW + AGAIN THE CIVILIZED WORLD IS GIVEN A RARE OPPORTUNITY TO VEIW MAN IN HIS PRIMAL STATE!! FOR EXAMPLE:
THE DOUGHNUT-BOY of SEATTLE, WASH.
THROUGHOUT HISTORY, SCIENTISTS HAVE AGONIZED OVER THE AWFUL QUESTION OF HUMAN NATURE---- DOES IT EXIST?? ARE WE BORN WITH THE DESIRE TO GET A JOB AND EAT TWINKIES, OR IS THIS A LEARNED CONDITION??? AND WHAT ABOUT HOW WE BRED WIENER DOGS TO LOOK THAT WAY???
LOST OR ABANDONED IN THE HOSTESS FACTORY IN SEATTLES INDUSTRIAL NEIGHBORHOOD, "LITTLE DUNKIN'" SOMEHOW SURVIVED ----- FOR 9 YEARS!
COMEEK de LYNDA BARRY ©81

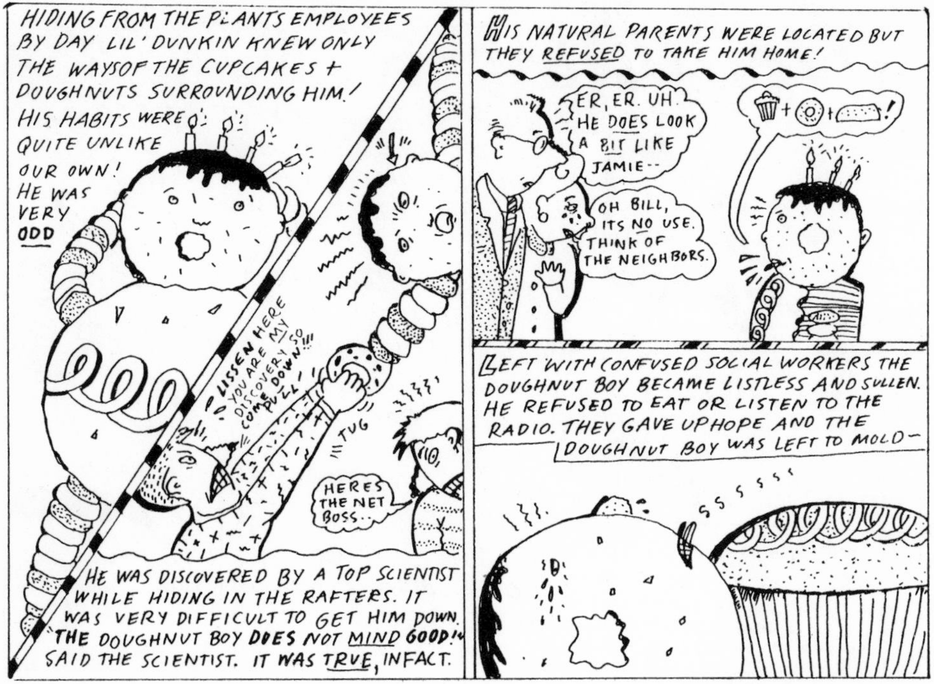
HIDING FROM THE PLANTS EMPLOYEES BY DAY LIL' DUNKIN KNEW ONLY THE WAYS OF THE CUPCAKES + DOUGHNUTS SURROUNDING HIM!
HIS HABITS WERE QUITE UNLIKE OUR OWN! HE WAS VERY ODD
LISSEN HERE YOU ARE MY DISCOVERY SO COME DOWN!!!
PULL
TUG
HERES THE NET BOSS..
HE WAS DISCOVERED BY A TOP SCIENTIST WHILE HIDING IN THE RAFTERS. IT WAS VERY DIFFICULT TO GET HIM DOWN. "THE DOUGHNUT BOY DOES NOT MIND GOOD!" SAID THE SCIENTIST. IT WAS TRUE, INFACT.
HIS NATURAL PARENTS WERE LOCATED BUT THEY REFUSED TO TAKE HIM HOME!
ER, ER. UH. HE DOES LOOK A BIT LIKE JAMIE--
OH BILL, ITS NO USE. THINK OF THE NEIGHBORS.
LEFT WITH CONFUSED SOCIAL WORKERS THE DOUGHNUT BOY BECAME LISTLESS AND SULLEN. HE REFUSED TO EAT OR LISTEN TO THE RADIO. THEY GAVE UP HOPE AND THE DOUGHNUT BOY WAS LEFT TO MOLD—

continued

NEW10 YEARS

YOU BETTER STAND EVERY BODY DO YOU

DAILY DA

1892

EVERYONE FIGHTING WITH EVERY ONE ELSE I'LOVE

DOG GONE! WELL HELLO THERE YOU. YOU'RE COMIN' WITH ME NOW

A DOCTOR FROM OHIO READ ABOUT THE CASE IN THE NEWS- PAPER AND FLEW THERE F= A= S= T

THEY GLADLY GAVE UP LIL' DUNKIN AND THE DOCTOR FLEW HIM TO OHIO FOR TESTS.

IN A SPECIAL NEWS CONFERENCE THE DOCTOR ANNOUNCED ---

ACCORDING TO MYSELF, THIS SO CALLED "DOUGHNUT BOY" IS NO DIFFERENT THAN ANY BODY ELSE! AND THIS IS JUST A MEANS OF GETTING ATTENTION AND HAVING AN EXCUSE TO AVOID GETTING A JOB!! BUT IT WON'T WORK. AT LEAST NOT IN AMERICA! I'VE CONTACTED MR. HIX AT THE DOWNTOWN SEARS. HE SAYS HE NEEDS A YOUNG CLERK! NO MORE FREE LUNCH FOR THIS KID, BY GOLLY!

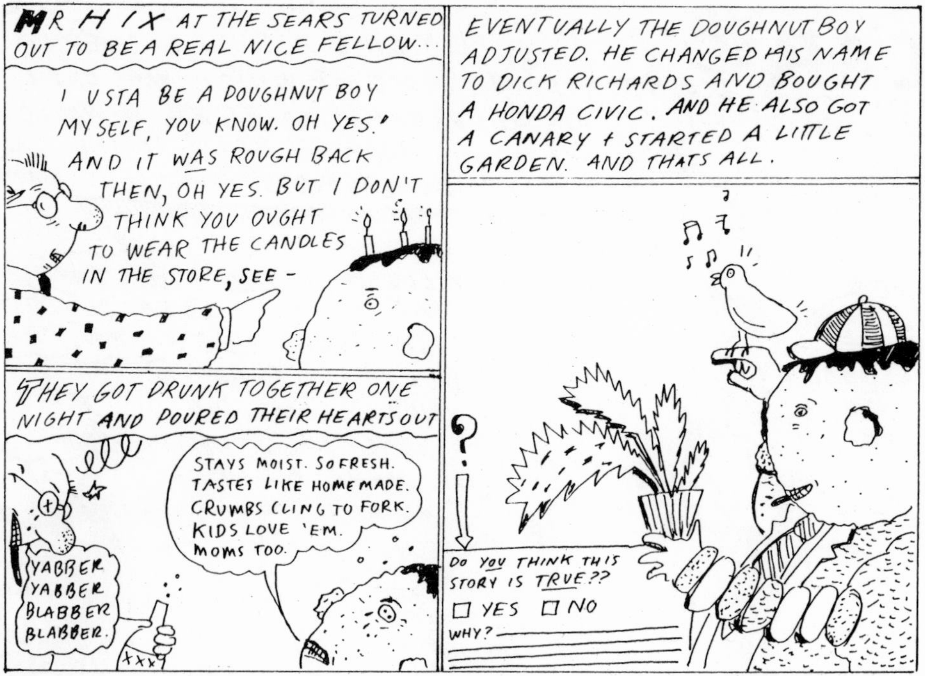
MR HIX AT THE SEARS TURNED OUT TO BE A REAL NICE FELLOW...
I USTA BE A DOUGHNUT BOY MYSELF, YOU KNOW. OH YES! AND IT WAS ROUGH BACK THEN, OH YES. BUT I DON'T THINK YOU OUGHT TO WEAR THE CANDLES IN THE STORE, SEE -
THEY GOT DRUNK TOGETHER ONE NIGHT AND POURED THEIR HEARTS OUT
YABBER YABBER BLABBER BLABBER.
STAYS MOIST. SO FRESH. TASTES LIKE HOMEMADE. CRUMBS CLING TO FORK. KIDS LOVE 'EM. MOMS TOO.
XXX
EVENTUALLY THE DOUGHNUT BOY ADJUSTED. HE CHANGED HIS NAME TO DICK RICHARDS AND BOUGHT A HONDA CIVIC. AND HE ALSO GOT A CANARY + STARTED A LITTLE GARDEN. AND THATS ALL.
?
DO YOU THINK THIS STORY IS TRUE??
☐ YES ☐ NO
WHY?

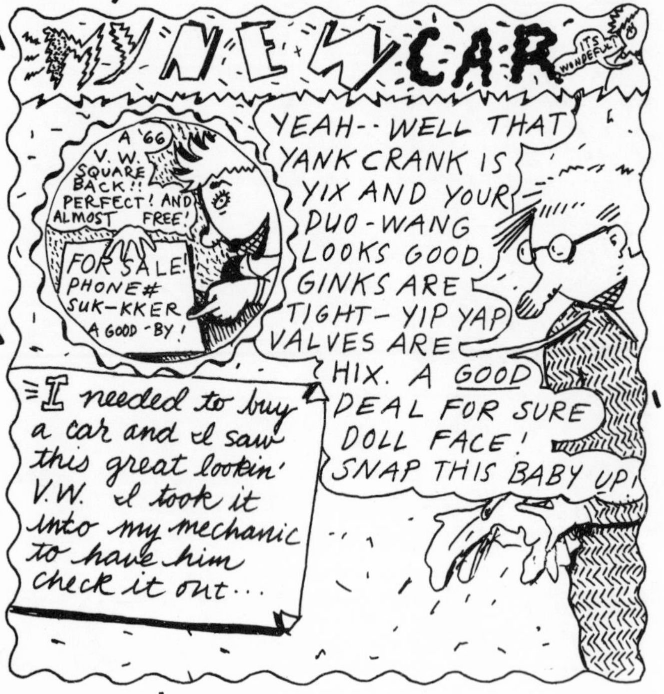
MY NEW CAR
ITS WONDEFUL!
A '66 V.W. SQUARE BACK!! PERFECT! AND ALMOST FREE!
FOR SALE! PHONE# SUK-KKER A GOOD-BY!
I needed to buy a car and I saw this great lookin' V.W. I took it into my mechanic to have him check it out...
YEAH--WELL THAT YANK CRANK IS YIX AND YOUR DUO-WANG LOOKS GOOD. GINKS ARE TIGHT–YIP YAP VALVES ARE HIX. A GOOD DEAL FOR SURE DOLL FACE! SNAP THIS BABY UP!

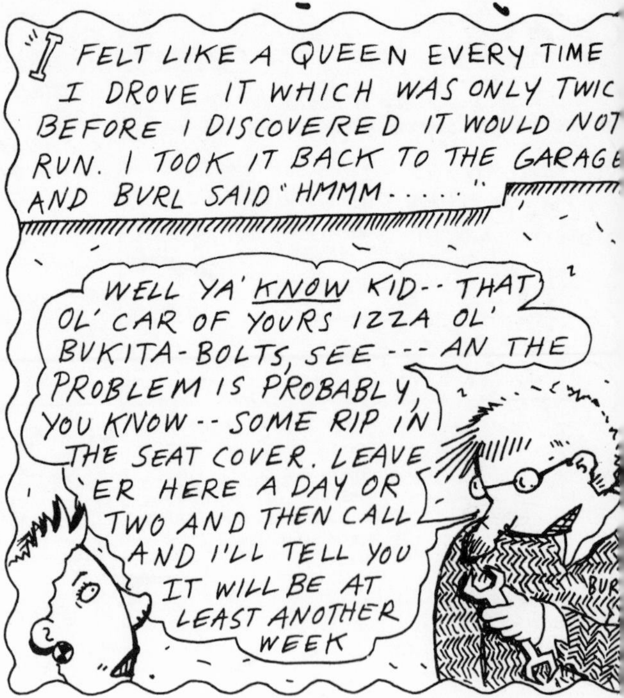
I FELT LIKE A QUEEN EVERY TIME I DROVE IT WHICH WAS ONLY TWIC BEFORE I DISCOVERED IT WOULD NOT RUN. I TOOK IT BACK TO THE GARAGE AND BURL SAID "HMMM....."
WELL YA' KNOW KID--THAT OL' CAR OF YOURS IZZA OL' BUKITA-BOLTS, SEE---AN THE PROBLEM IS PROBABLY, YOU KNOW--SOME RIP IN THE SEAT COVER. LEAVE 'ER HERE A DAY OR TWO AND THEN CALL AND I'LL TELL YOU IT WILL BE AT LEAST ANOTHER WEEK

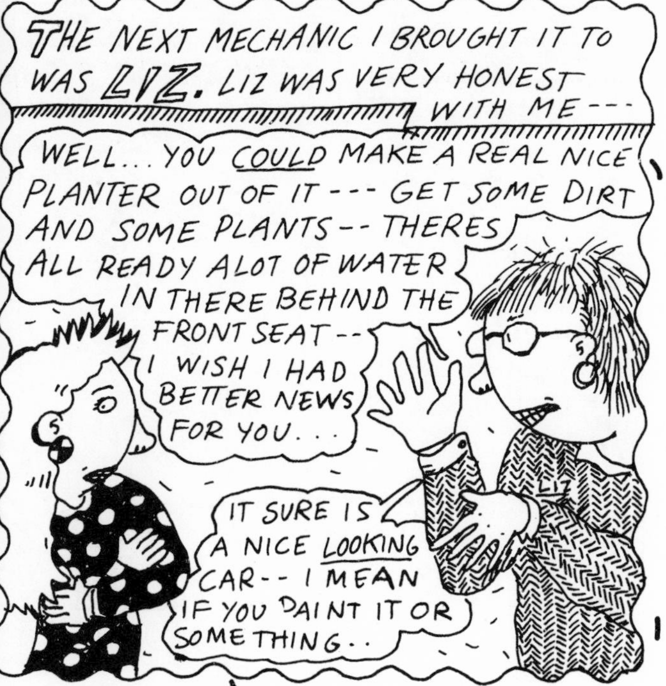
THE NEXT MECHANIC I BROUGHT IT TO WAS LIZ. LIZ WAS VERY HONEST WITH ME---
WELL... YOU COULD MAKE A REAL NICE PLANTER OUT OF IT --- GET SOME DIRT AND SOME PLANTS -- THERES ALL READY ALOT OF WATER IN THERE BEHIND THE FRONT SEAT -- I WISH I HAD BETTER NEWS FOR YOU...
IT SURE IS A NICE LOOKING CAR -- I MEAN IF YOU PAINT IT OR SOMETHING..
LIZ

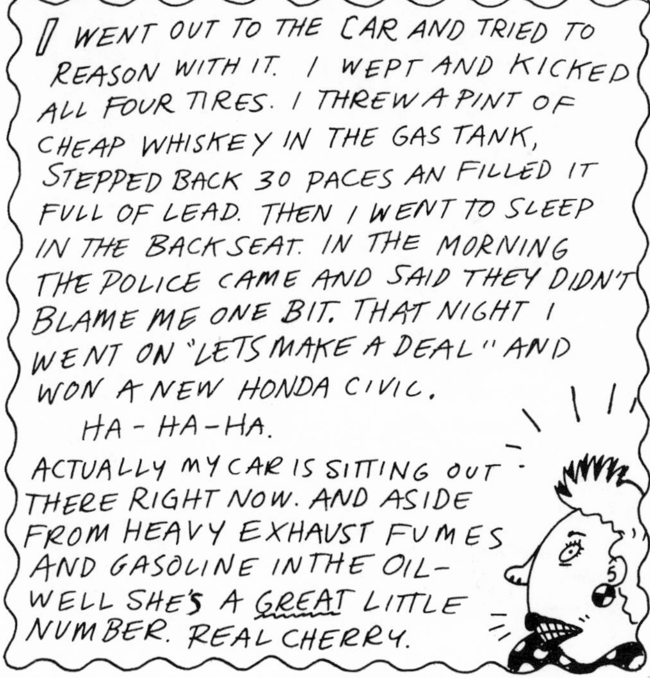
I WENT OUT TO THE CAR AND TRIED TO REASON WITH IT. I WEPT AND KICKED ALL FOUR TIRES. I THREW A PINT OF CHEAP WHISKEY IN THE GAS TANK, STEPPED BACK 30 PACES AN FILLED IT FULL OF LEAD. THEN I WENT TO SLEEP IN THE BACK SEAT. IN THE MORNING THE POLICE CAME AND SAID THEY DIDN'T BLAME ME ONE BIT. THAT NIGHT I WENT ON "LETS MAKE A DEAL" AND WON A NEW HONDA CIVIC.
HA-HA-HA.
ACTUALLY MY CAR IS SITTING OUT THERE RIGHT NOW. AND ASIDE FROM HEAVY EXHAUST FUMES AND GASOLINE IN THE OIL- WELL SHE'S A GREAT LITTLE NUMBER. REAL CHERRY.

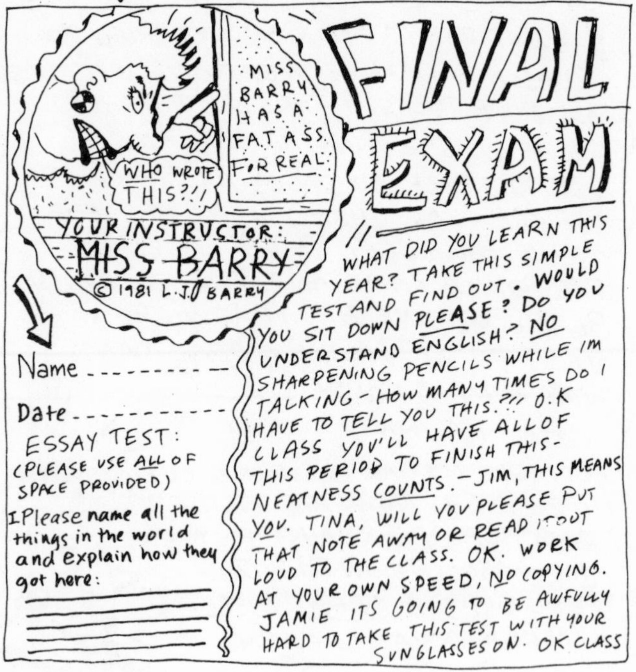

FINAL EXAM
MISS BARRY HAS A FAT ASS FOR REAL
WHO WROTE THIS?!!
YOUR INSTRUCTOR: MISS BARRY
© 1981 L.J. BARRY
Name
Date
ESSAY TEST:
(PLEASE USE ALL OF SPACE PROVIDED)
I Please name all the things in the world and explain how they got here:
WHAT DID YOU LEARN THIS YEAR? TAKE THIS SIMPLE TEST AND FIND OUT. WOULD YOU SIT DOWN PLEASE? DO YOU UNDERSTAND ENGLISH? NO SHARPENING PENCILS WHILE IM TALKING - HOW MANY TIMES DO I HAVE TO TELL YOU THIS?!! O.K CLASS YOU'LL HAVE ALL OF THIS PERIOD TO FINISH THIS - NEATNESS COUNTS. - JIM, THIS MEANS YOU. TINA, WILL YOU PLEASE PUT THAT NOTE AWAY OR READ IT OUT LOUD TO THE CLASS. OK. WORK AT YOUR OWN SPEED, NO COPYING. JAMIE ITS GOING TO BE AWFULLY HARD TO TAKE THIS TEST WITH YOUR SUNGLASSES ON. OK CLASS

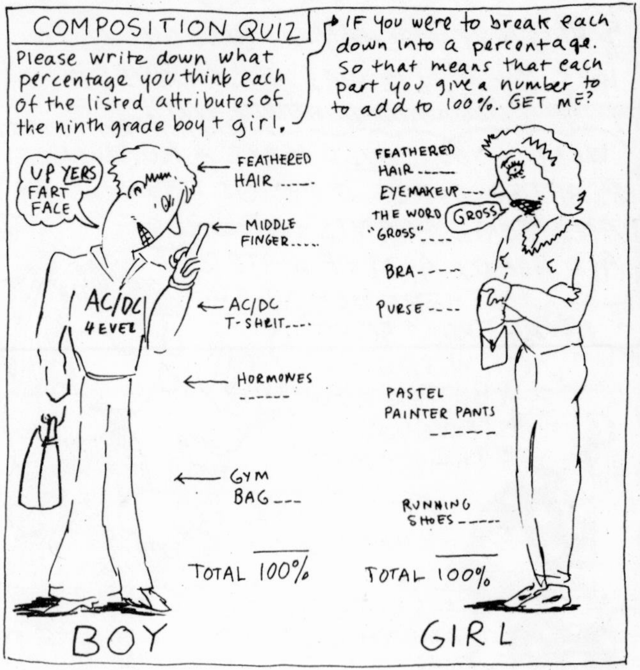

COMPOSITION QUIZ
Please write down what percentage you think each of the listed attributes of the ninth grade boy + girl.
IF you were to break each down into a percentage. So that means that each part you give a number to to add to 100%. GET ME?
UP YERS FART FACE
FEATHERED HAIR
MIDDLE FINGER
AC/DC 4 EVER
AC/DC T-SHIRT
HORMONES
GYM BAG
TOTAL 100%
BOY
FEATHERED HAIR
EYEMAKEUP
THE WORD "GROSS"
GROSS
BRA
PURSE
PASTEL PAINTER PANTS
RUNNING SHOES
TOTAL 100%
GIRL

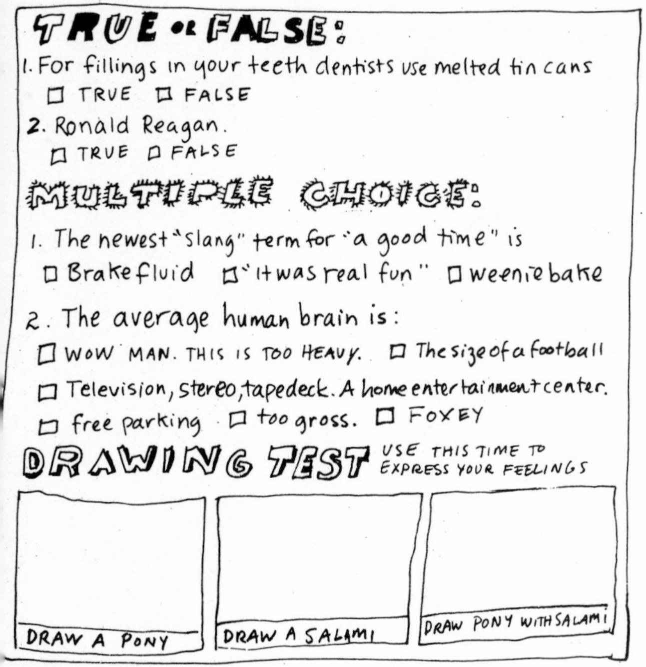
TRUE OR FALSE:
1. For fillings in your teeth dentists use melted tin cans
☐ TRUE ☐ FALSE
2. Ronald Reagan.
☐ TRUE ☐ FALSE
MULTIPLE CHOICE:
1. The newest "slang" term for "a good time" is
☐ Brake fluid ☐ "It was real fun" ☐ weenie bake
2. The average human brain is:
☐ WOW MAN. THIS IS TOO HEAVY. ☐ The size of a football
☐ Television, stereo, tapedeck. A home entertainment center.
☐ free parking ☐ too gross. ☐ FOXEY
DRAWING TEST
USE THIS TIME TO EXPRESS YOUR FEELINGS
DRAW A PONY
DRAW A SALAMI
DRAW PONY WITH SALAMI

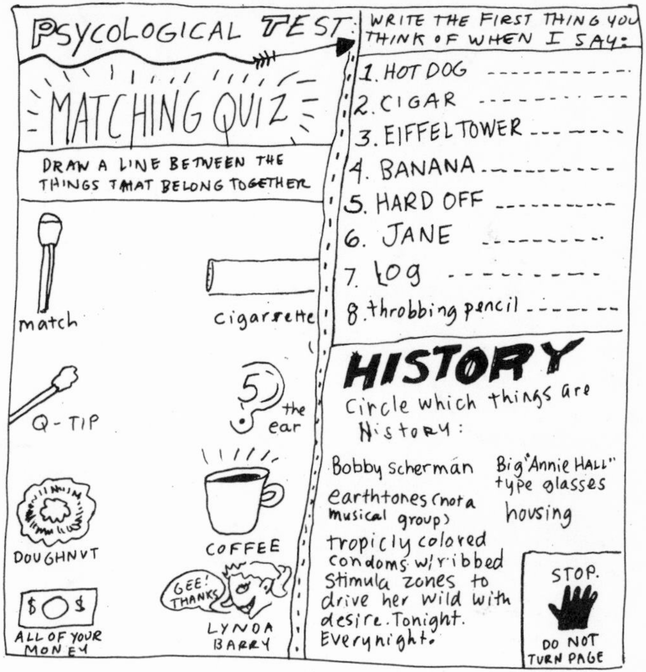
PSYCOLOGICAL TEST:
WRITE THE FIRST THING YOU THINK OF WHEN I SAY:
1. HOT DOG
2. CIGAR
3. EIFFEL TOWER
4. BANANA
5. HARD OFF
6. JANE
7. LOG
8. throbbing pencil
MATCHING QUIZ
DRAW A LINE BETWEEN THE THINGS THAT BELONG TOGETHER
match
cigarrette
Q-TIP
the ear
DOUGHNUT
COFFEE
$ $
ALL OF YOUR MONEY
GEE! THANKS
LYNDA BARRY
HISTORY
Circle which things are History:
Bobby Scherman
Big "Annie HALL" type glasses
earthtones (not a musical group)
housing
tropicly colored condoms w/ribbed stimula zones to drive her wild with desire. Tonight. Everynight.
STOP.
DO NOT TURN PAGE

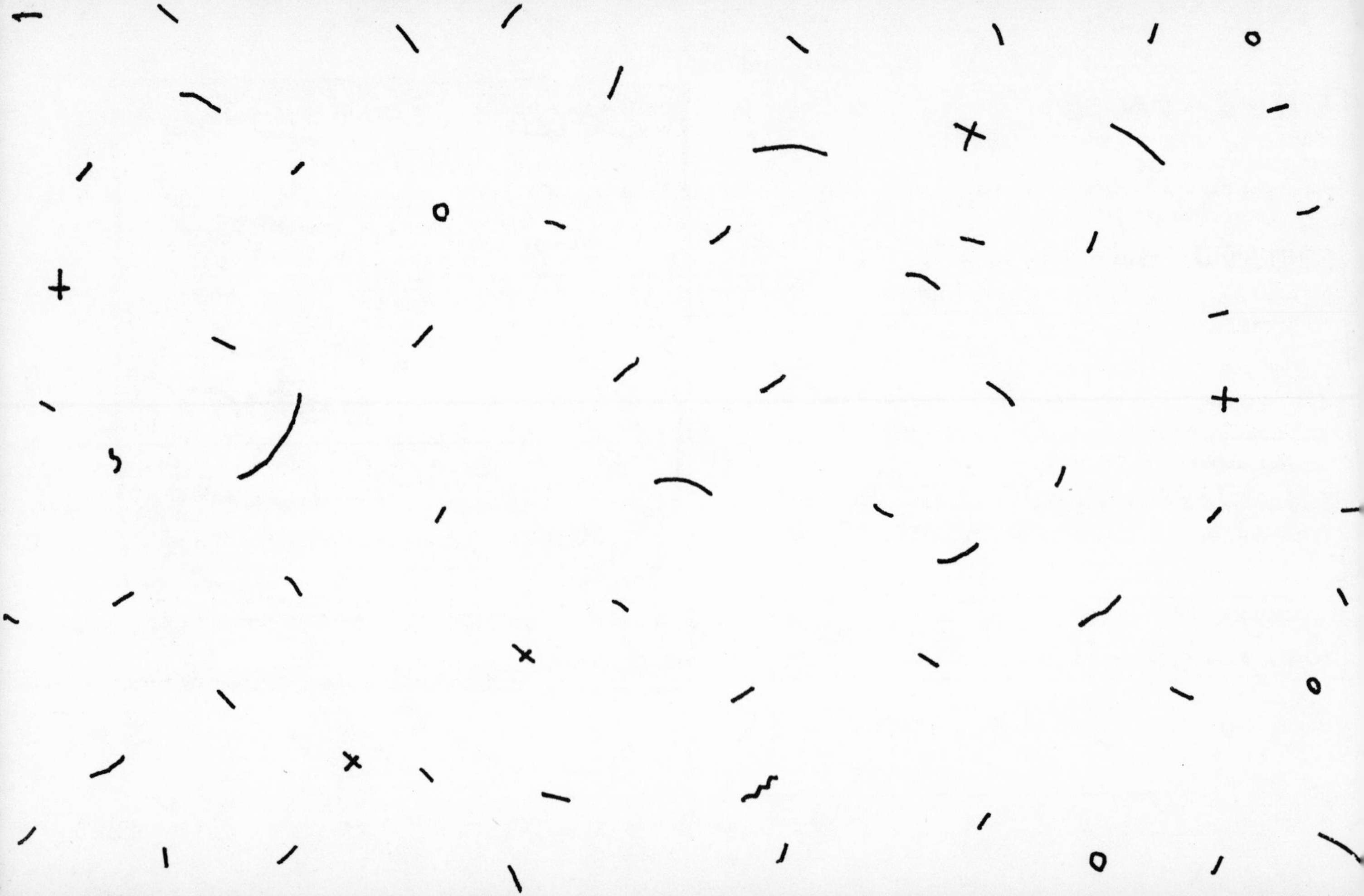

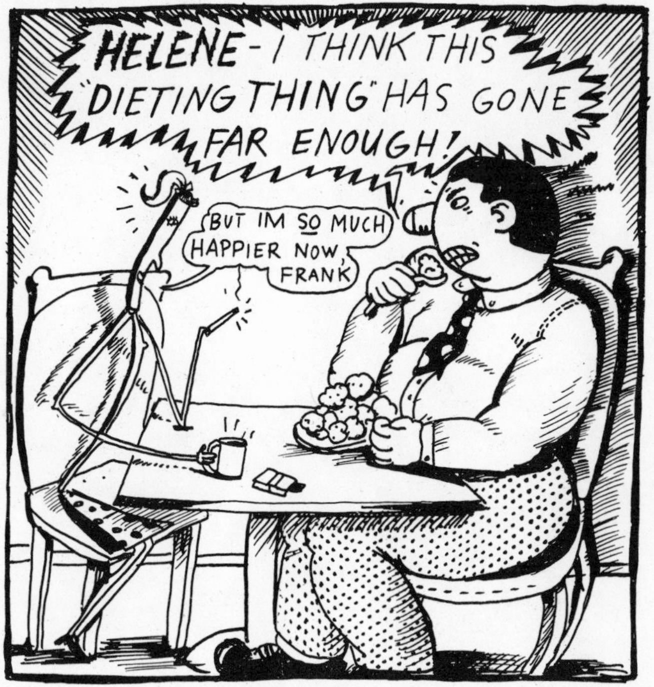
HELENE - I THINK THIS "DIETING THING" HAS GONE FAR ENOUGH!
BUT IM SO MUCH HAPPIER NOW, FRANK

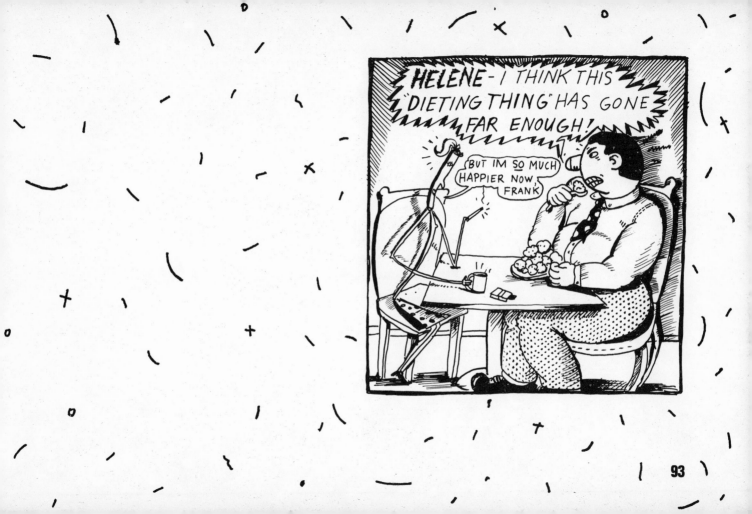

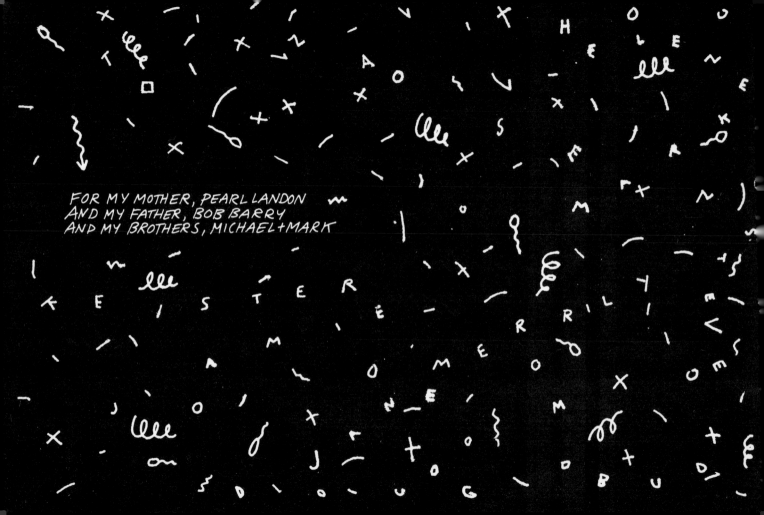

FOR MY MOTHER, PEARL LANDON
AND MY FATHER, BOB BARRY
AND MY BROTHERS, MICHAEL+MARK

PHOTO BY DIRK PARK

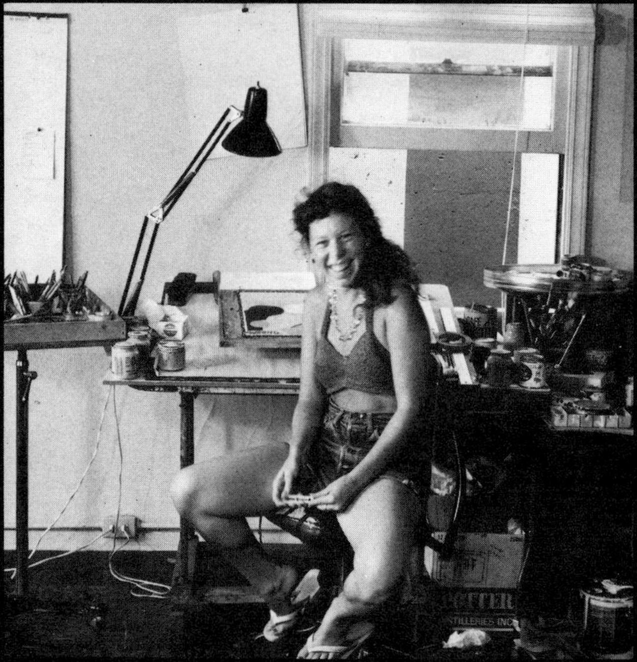

SUMMER 1981

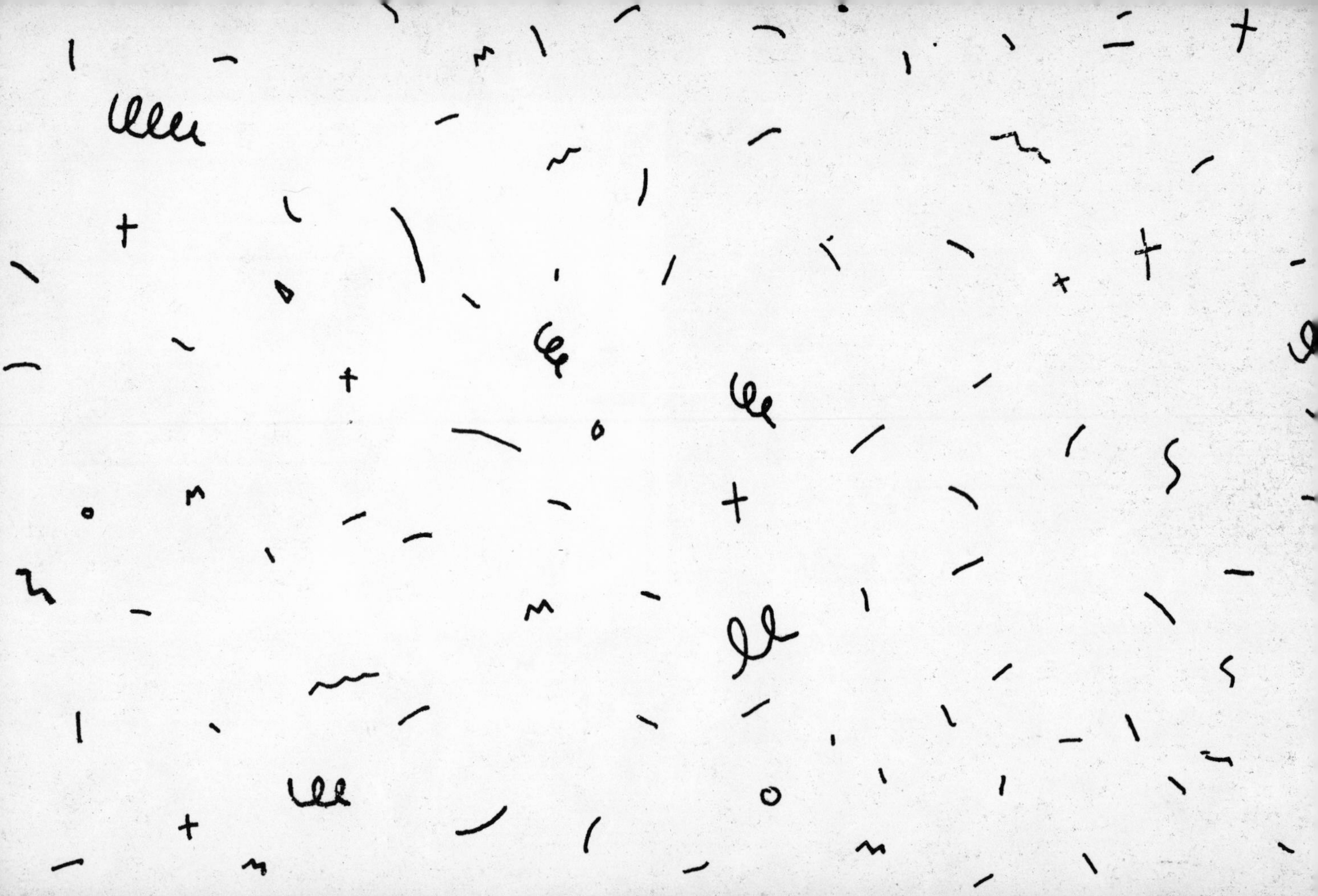